Zenobia

Nick Dear's theatre credits include *The Art of Success* (a portrait of the artist William Hogarth) at the Royal Shakespeare Company and subsequently at Manhattan Theatre Club, New York. It won him the John Whiting Award for 1986, and he was nominated for Laurence Olivier Awards for both this and *A Family Affair*. He was Playwright in Residence at the Royal Exchange, Manchester in 1987–8. Other plays include *The Last Days of Don Juan* (after Tirso de Molina; RSC, 1990); *In the Ruins* (Royal Court, 1990); *Food of Love* (Almeida, 1988); *A Family Affair* (after Ostrovsky; Cheek by Jowl, 1988); and *Temptation* (RSC, 1984). He has written the libretti for two operas, *A Family Affair* (1993) and *Siren Song* (1994), both premièred at the Almeida Opera Festival. His first feature film screenplay, Jane Austen's *Persuasion*, was shown on BBC TV in 1995. He has also written extensively for radio.

NICK DEAR

Zenobia

faber and faber
LONDON · BOSTON

First published in Great Britain in 1995 by
Faber and Faber Limited, 3 Queen Square London WC1N 3AU

Photoset by Parker Typesetting Service, Leicester
Printed in England by Clays Ltd, St Ives plc

© Nick Dear, 1995

Nick Dear is hereby identified as translator of this work in accordance with
Section 77 of the Copyright, Designs and Patents Act 1988.

All professional and amateur rights in this play are strictly reserved and
applications for permission to perform it must be made in advance to
Rosica Colin Ltd, 1 Clareville Grove Mews, London SW7 5AH

A CIP record for this book
is available from the British Library

ISBN 0-571-17676-3

2 4 6 8 10 9 7 5 3 1

In their essentials the historical events described are true.

The quotations from 'On the Sublime' are taken from *Classical Literary Criticism*, translated by T. S. Dorsch (with kind permission of Penguin Books); and I must acknowledge my debt to Richard Stoneman's book *Palmyra and its Empire*, published by the University of Michigan Press.

Nick Dear

Characters

Odainat King of Palmyra
Hairan His Son
Moqimu A Waiter
Worod A General
Longinus A Philosopher
Wahballat Son of Zenobia
Timagenes A Statesman
Yedibel A Clerk
Zenobia Queen of Palmyra
Malik A Eunuch
Zabdas Commander of the Palmyrene Army
Porphyry A Student of Philosophy
Quintinius A Roman Senator
Gratus A Roman Senator
Aurelian Emperor of Rome
Probus His Tribune
Pertinax A Roman General
Bedouin Scout
A Roman Prefect
Cato Roman Soldier
Antoninus Roman Soldier
Philip Roman Soldier
Syrus Roman Soldier
Dawkins An Explorer
Wood An Explorer

Roman Soldiers, Generals
and Courtiers

The play begins in Syria AD 267.

Zenobia was first performed at the Young Vic on 2 August 1995. The cast, in order of appearance, was as follows:

Odainat Colin Farrell
Hairan James Barriscale
Moqimu Stephen Clyde
Worod Gregor Singleton
Longinus Robert Gillespie
Wahballat James Frain
Timagenes David Beames
Yedibel Colin Starkey
Zenobia Penny Downie
Malik Clive Rowe
Zabdas Conrad Asquith
Porphyry Emily Raymond
Quintinius Gwynn Beech
Gratus Arthur Cox
Aurelian Trevor Cooper
Probus Sean O'Callaghan
Pertinax David Hounslow
Bedouin Scout Quill Roberts
Roman Prefect Colin Farrell
Cato James Barriscale
Antoninus Gregor Singleton
Philip Gwynn Beech
Syrus Darren Roberts
Dawkins Quill Roberts
Wood Darren Roberts

Roman Soldiers, Generals, Palmyrene Soldiers and **Courtiers** played by members of the cast and Joanne Howarth.

Directed by Mike Ockrent
Designed by Tim Goodchild
Lighting designed by Bob Bryan
Music by Jonathan Dove

An RSC/Young Vic Co-production.

Part One

SCENE ONE

A camp in the Syrian desert, AD 267. *The tent of the King,* **Odainat.** *He is with his son,* **Hairan,** *a soldier. They are coming to the end of a feast. Odainat pats his stomach.*

Odainat Food tastes different when a war is won. There is no churning cauldron in your gut, that must be quelled before you start to eat. No haste, no fear this mouthful is your last. You may pick discriminately at your dinner, savouring each delicacy with the tip of your tongue. The first meal of the peace – every flavour is a blessing – every crumb an answered prayer. And my feast I share with my firstborn; and that too gives me joy.

Odainat's hands fall on a cochlis brooch that pins his tunic together. He removes it and pins it to Hairan's tunic.

This is one of our finest royal jewels.

Hairan Thank you, father.

Odainat It was given to me by my wife.

Hairan Then you should –

Odainat No, keep it. You fought well. You deserve it. Four days' march, and we're home. I have sent Zabdas ahead to announce our victories.

Hairan You will enter the city in triumph.

Odainat I left it Odainat, a son of the desert. I return Odenathus, friend of Rome, Protector of the East. I am satisfied.

A valet, **Moqimu***, brings a large jug of wine and glasses.*

What is that, Moqimu?

Moqimu Wine, Majesty.

Odainat We have no wine.

Moqimu A gift, Majesty, from the Roman Commander at Emesa.

Odainat The Romans send us wine? We *have* done well today! (*laughing*) Drink with me, Hairan. Drink a toast: to home!

Moqimu pours wine and exits, leaving the jug behind.

Hairan To Palmyra!

They drink. Odainat toasts again.

Odainat To the Queen!

Odainat drinks. Hairan hesitates.

She will never replace your mother, I know that. But have the courtesy to show respect where it is due.

Hairan (*drinks grudgingly*) To your wife.

Odainat My wife . . . like a glittering star, lighting up the night of my old age. Her eyes as dark as a raven's wing; her teeth so white, they seem inlaid with pearls. How I cherish her.

Hairan The soldiers say she never lets you in her bed, father.

Odainat I have with her five children.

Hairan Five visits only, they say.

Odainat Envy breeds malice in a body of men.

Hairan I would be ashamed, to have such a reputation.

2

Odainat You are sour tonight.

Hairan Forgive me. I miss the war. Peace brings a dreadful silence. I miss the clatter of swords . . . the whisper of arrows . . .

Odainat Then drink: to the noise of battle.

Hairan To Persian blood in the dust!

> *They drink, and laugh.* **Worod**, *a general, enters escorting* **Longinus**, *who carries a travelling bag. He kneels before the King.*

Who is this?

Worod A scholar. Says he got lost.

Longinus I am Cassius Longinus, Majesty, of Athens. I travel to Palmyra.

Odainat Palmyra? On what business?

Longinus Philosophy, my Lord. With some Greek, a little rhetoric, a parcel of mathematics. Sophistry, disputation, the Emanation of the Universal Mind. And I can read and write.

Worod (*laughs*) A joker.

Hairan Kick him out.

Longinus No no, I have a letter! A formal invitation to attend the court of Queen Zenobia, and tutor her son!

Odainat (*reads the letter*) It is my wife's hand. (*smiles*) Wahballat wants to take up philosophy.

Hairan Wahballat is a girl. He should take up knitting.

Odainat (*to Longinus*) My sons . . . are as alike as wormwood and syrup.

Longinus It is rare indeed to find all the great qualities

3

conjoined in one man's form, Majesty. Perhaps your soul is too capacious for your seed, and must, therefore, subdivide itself?

Odainat (*laughs*) No. They had different mothers. Sit with us.

Longinus and Worod sit down. Longinus won't accept the proffered glass of wine.

Longinus I regret I cannot take wine.

Odainat No wine?

Hairan Why not?

Longinus It impedes the trajectory of logic. To launch a thought, to see it fly, to watch it arc gracefully and land with a thud in another man's brain – that is my one pleasure. Fill me up with wine, and all my best ideas buzz hither and yon like a nest of hornets, impressively voluble but in the end quite devoid of purpose. I'll have a cup of milk if you've got one.

Worod The ass wants milk.

Worod and Hairan laugh. But Odainat is thoughtful.

Odainat You reason well, Longinus. Let us all drink milk!

Hairan You cannot drink milk tonight. Tonight you are a soldier.

Worod Tonight you are a hero.

Odainat (*warmly*) Worod, thank you.

The three of them clash their glasses and drain them. Longinus watches.

Longinus (*cautiously*) May I enquire – the bodies strewn across the landscape – whose they are?

Hairan Persians.

Longinus . . . And is that good or bad?

Worod You are new to the East?

Longinus Fresh off the boat.

Worod But you do know who the Emperor of Rome is?

Longinus looks puzzled for a moment, then rummages in his bag for a coin.

Longinus Unless something terrible has happened, it's . . . (*He peers at the head on the coin.*) . . . Valerian. But they come and go at such a lick, don't they?

Worod Something terrible has happened.

Longinus Ah.

Worod Valerian was taken prisoner by the Persians, who rose against him. Their leader used him as a footstool for his horse, then cut the flesh off the Emperor, and had him tanned and stuffed.

Hairan gives a little involuntary grunt, and puts his hand to his stomach, grimacing.

Odainat What is it?

Hairan Rich food.

Worod The Empire itself was in danger. My Lord Odainat, an illustrious King of Syria and loyal subject of the new Emperor Gallienus, answered the call with seventy thousand tribesmen. Those Persian corpses are the outcome. We have restored the Empire in the East. We are the heroes of Palmyra!

Odainat Ever visited Palmyra?

Longinus Never.

Odainat You have delights in store. It is a miracle in stone. I long to see my wife again, to walk with her through the colonnades.

Hairan That's about all you'll be doing.

Odainat (*ignores Hairan; to Longinus*) With this banquet we welcome the return of peace to our region. We won a great battle today. There will be no more fighting.

Worod (*to Odainat*) You are made a Roman Consul, so I hear.

Longinus A Consul? From a small city-state in the desert? It would seem to me, in my ignorance of matters political, that that is some achievement.

Odainat Palmyra is no mud-hut enclave round a stagnant pool, Longinus. It is a union of tribes. We rule from the Great Sea to the Parthian border. And thus control the trade routes, east to west. We are rich beyond imagination.

Hairan Yet you can't buy a kiss from your wife.

> *Odainat raises his arm – from nowhere a dagger has appeared in his hand. Worod catches his arm. Stools are overturned.*

Odainat You dare insult the Queen once more!

Hairan You prefer her to me! I am the first in blood, yet you prefer her and her litter!

Odainat You will show respect!

Hairan Respect? When I am King of Palmyra – your widow will show respect!

> *Hairan throws to the floor the brooch that Odainat gave him and leaves the tent. Worod pours more drinks.*

6

Worod He will learn to be a statesman.

The King is morose. He drinks hard.

Odainat (*to Longinus*) Have you sons?

Longinus No. But I have a pupil. He is just as bad.

Odainat gives an involuntary burp and clutches at his stomach.

Odainat What did we eat?

Worod Ostrich.

Odainat That'll be it. (*to Longinus*) Don't judge Hairan too harshly. Can't be easy for the boy. His mother died in childbirth. A year later I found a girl of noble blood, but wild and wilful – radiant, but difficult. I tamed her. Taught her dignity. The Queen she has become surpasses every wonder of the world, ancient or modern, take your pick. But nothing I can do will make her love my son and heir. Her own boy she dotes on and pampers.

Longinus Oh, that is quite natural.

Odainat Is it?

Longinus I have little experience of women – well, none, to be perfectly frank – but they surely all promote their offspring, and resent another's claim?

Odainat Yes, petty jealousies they nibble at like nuts, to dull their appetite for power. I bear no grudge – he is our son – but how do I content her?

Longinus Flatter her. Indulge her. Lay siege to her with presents.

Odainat Good, Longinus. The fortune I won in the war, I will lavish on her! She will live in luxury, the wife of a Consul –

Longinus I'm sure that's all she's ever wanted.

Odainat – and Wahballat shall have his philosophy. I may even dabble myself.

Odainat and Longinus laugh. Worod falls off his seat and has convulsions on the floor.

Worod!

Worod Where did you get the wine?

Longinus What is it?

Odainat The wine?

Worod Poison!

Odainat is stunned. He remains very still, hands on his stomach.

Odainat Not the ostrich . . . ?

Worod (*gasps with pain*) I didn't eat it!

Hairan crashes into the tent, reeling and vomiting.

Hairan What's wrong with me?

Odainat Poison.

Hairan I am poisoned?

Odainat (*to Longinus*) You?

Longinus I'm afraid I feel quite all right.

Worod The wine! Where did you get it?

Hairan Sent by the Romans.

Worod Treason!

Hairan Father, I am dying! (*He groans.*)

Worod We saved them! And this is how they thank us . . . (*He dies.*)

Longinus Majesty . . . ?

Odainat Yes, I can feel it. The trickle of eternity. Good subject for an ode, Longinus. Disillusion of a King at the hour of his death.

Hairan Father – forgive me. (*He dies.*)

Odainat Hairan . . . ?

Odainat sinks to his knees and crawls to his son's body.

At least he thought it was the work of Rome.

Longinus I'm sorry?

Odainat This wine came from my wife.

Longinus (*shocked*) How do you – ?

Odainat Sweetened with honey. Only she knows my taste. Now it is racing, racing through my veins. My guts like a blizzard of broken glass, kicked up by horses' hooves. A bear's claw lodged in my heart. (*He collapses.*) Now she has got what she must have desired. Her son on Palmyra's throne. (*He has convulsions.*) Where am I going, philosopher?

Longinus To join with the oneness of all matter . . .

Odainat Oh, Zenobia . . .

Odainat has convulsions and dies.

Longinus . . . I think. (*He takes stock.*) A king, a prince and a general, dead at one's feet. What are the logical consequences of such a proposition? Exactly. No amount of rhetoric can avert a catastrophe, no erudition shield my innocence from angry spears and swords. My training affords a clear grasp of the available options. One could ruminate at some length on the false grandeur

9

of kingship and the levelling blade of time. Or one could run.

Longinus grabs his bag and goes to leave. He passes the jewelled brooch that Hairan threw to the floor. He picks it up and hides it in his cloak. He runs out. A pause. Moqimu enters and sees the bodies. He puts his hand to Odainat's heart. Nothing. He bangs his jug loudly against his tray.

SCENE TWO

Palmyra. A palace. A procession enters, in funeral attire. At its head is **Wahballat,** *a teenage boy, followed by a statesman,* **Timagenes,** *and* **Yedibel,** *his clerk. Behind them come more* **Statesmen** *and* **Courtiers.** *Wahballat slumps wearily on the throne and shuts his eyes. Cautiously, Timagenes and Yedibel approach him, with documents.*

Timagenes The tariffs, Majesty?

Wahballat So soon?

Timagenes We need the Royal Assent.

Wahballat I have just buried my father . . . !

Timagenes It is the height of the season, and four separate caravans are approaching the city. The annual increase falls due. Any delay means a massive loss of revenue.

Wahballat If you put the tariffs up, won't the traders simply go another way?

Timagenes There is no other way. Every oasis between the Euphrates and the sea is under our dominion.

Wahballat You can do what you jolly well like, then, can't you, Timagenes?

Timagenes You must approve it. Please let my clerk read the proposals.

Yedibel (*reads from a papyrus scroll*) Aromatic oils in alabaster, per camel load, from 25 to 30 denarii; aromatic oils in goatskin, per camel load, from 13 to 15 denarii; bales of silk, per donkey load, from 40 to 50 denarii; bales –

Wahballat All right, all right!

He takes the official seal which Timagenes offers him and stamps the document. In the background **Zenobia**, *veiled with a headscarf, so that only her eyes can be seen and wearing flowing robes, emerges from the procession with her escort, the eunuch* **Malik**. *He fans her with a palm frond as she watches her son.*

Seems an awful lot of money just to pass through the city.

Timagenes We have water, Majesty. Water commands high prices. Now, as to the matter of the new pediment upon the Temple of Baalshamin –

Yedibel unrolls another scroll. Wahballat leaps from his throne in frustration.

Wahballat Look here, I don't care about your pediments! My mother is in charge of public works. Why can't you leave me in peace?

Timagenes Because you are King, Wahballat.

Wahballat I never asked to be King! Hairan should be King!

Timagenes Hairan is dead.

Zenobia Hairan is – regrettably – dead.

Zenobia comes forward. The Statesmen bow.

Wahballat Speak to the Queen. Leave me to my books.

Wahballat finds his book in a corner and sits down to read.

Zenobia You have attended to the tariffs?

They show her the scroll. She glances over it, checking figures.

Not enough. Not enough. Not enough.

Yedibel Not enough, Majesty?

Zenobia Raise them further.

Timagenes We are in surplus already. Any more and the Roman officials will take steps.

Zenobia Steps, Timagenes? Steps? I don't know where you have been this afternoon but I have been in the Valley of the Tombs, mourning my dear husband. I designed the vaults of his funeral tower. I did not think to see them used so soon. Who did this? Who stocked these rooms of death?

Timagenes The Romans, Majesty.

Yedibel The Romans.

Zenobia Yes. Odainat went to war on the westerners' behalf – and they killed him. Their meek client-king.

Timagenes We understand your bitterness. The nation shares your grief.

Yedibel The troops are enraged. They sing songs of revenge in their barracks.

Zenobia Then let us show our anger. Are we taxing our own people here? No, we are simply raising the price of saffron on the Via Piperatica. The Romans are addicted to their silks and scents and spices; life without black pepper would be simply inconceivable; so let them pay. Death duties.

Timagenes King Wahballat has already sealed the warrant.

Zenobia He is a minor! (*She rips up the document.*) Redraft it. Malik, show them out.

> *Timagenes and Yedibel leave with Malik. The Courtiers disperse. Zenobia goes to Wahballat and runs her hand through his hair.*

Zenobia You miss him, don't you?

Wahballat Why, don't you?

Zenobia I am saving my tears for my pillow. (*Pause.*) There is a gap, a void, in the nation. A space that must be filled.

Wahballat I don't have the qualifications.

Zenobia No. I haven't passed the exams, either. But are you not ambitious?

Wahballat Not awfully, no.

Zenobia Look. Money drops into our purses like sweat off a merchant's chin. This place we have built is unique. We could fill it with people of genius! Create a paradise on earth!

Wahballat But what if the trade-routes shift? Or the Romans go off pepper?

Zenobia (*thoughtfully*) That, we must prepare for.

Wahballat But how?

Zenobia . . . It intrigues me, the living muscle of power.

Wahballat It gives me a headache.

Zenobia (*smiles*) One day you will govern with wisdom and strength. Your glories will make five hundred years of Roman civilization look like footprints in the sand. But for now, devote yourself to study. I will act for you.

Wahballat . . . Did you love my father?

Zenobia Love him?

Wahballat Love him . . . as a man?

Zenobia You mean did I sleep with him? I bore him children. So I must have done. It is not a very interesting subject. But you I presume are obsessed, seventeen and obsessed, with the secrets of slippery bodies. (*laughing*) Have you thought of wrestling?

She grapples with him, but Wahballat is unwilling to play, and pulls away.

Wahballat No, mother!

Zenobia Oh, my darling . . . I hate this adulthood. Once I could do anything with you: hurl you in the air, or lay you down and suck your toes. Be my little boy again . . . kiss me like you used to.

Wahballat (*kissing her dutifully*) I don't like fighting.

Zenobia Nor did your father. But he did what he had to do.

Wahballat Yes, and look where it got him!

Zenobia Your father saved Rome from the Persians.

Wahballat Is that why they killed him? He was a threat?

Zenobia Well, he defeated an army they could not defeat –

Wahballat So if the Persians beat the Romans –

14

Zenobia And he beat the Persians –

Wahballat . . . So he was assassinated.

Zenobia These creatures are not fit to rule the world!
They kill for pleasure! They are savages in well-cut clothes,
drunk on barbaric spectacle and hollow victory parades –
for they win no victories! Their Empire is weak.

Wahballat It is nursed by centuries of power.

Zenobia It is a dream, conjured out of sleep, and the toil
of slaves; its leadership corrupt; its legions committed to
holding the north, where the Goths are streaming through
the mountains like goose-fat through your fingers. And,
look, the East lies undefended.

Wahballat What are you suggesting we do?

Zenobia I am not sure exactly. But perhaps we could . . .
prod them a little.

Wahballat Don't be hasty, mother.

Zenobia These murders are an insult. And we must
respond.

> *Malik enters with a* **Guard** *leading Longinus, who looks
> the worse for wear. Longinus prostrates himself before
> Zenobia.*

Longinus Great Regent of Palmyra!

Malik He was found by a patrol, wandering the camel-
trails. They would have brained him as a spy, but he
produced a letter.

> *Malik hands Longinus's letter to Zenobia.*

Zenobia The philosopher . . . ! What happened to you?
We have been waiting months.

Longinus I set out with a caravan, and was halfway here, when I witnessed a – calamitous – moment of inspiration. I took my pen and ink, and ran, far away, into the wilderness, among the rocks and crags. I lived on thorns and berries, roamed with the beasts of the desert, and immersed myself in thought. (*He hands her a tattered manuscript.*) Here is the fruit of my labours. I call it *On the Sublime*. I humbly dedicate it to you, Zenobia, supereminent Queen.

Zenobia That is gracious.

Longinus One could hardly arrive empty-handed.

Zenobia What does the manuscript contain?

Longinus It is the repository of all my best ideas on beauty.

Wahballat May I? (*He glances through the text.*)

Zenobia My son, Wahballat.

Longinus (*bowing*) Cassius Longinus, of Athens.

Wahballat You left Athens? For this place?

Longinus I am told the climate is good.

Wahballat For years I have longed to see Athens.

Longinus The German tribes are banging on the gates. It's not a good time for a visit.

Wahballat (*reading*) I say, this is very intriguing . . . All my books are out of date.

Longinus All mine I left behind. To be wiped on Gothic arses. Ah, books, books . . .

Wahballat Send for them.

Longinus All of them?

Wahballat We shall start a library.

Longinus It will be my pleasure to induct a seat of learning. Especially in such a magnificent setting. One would never have expected to find so glittering a metropolis in the desolate heart of Arabia.

Wahballat We have water. We grow twenty different kinds of date!

Longinus Do you really? Well, I never knew that. Twenty different kinds, eh?

Wahballat Yes, but they all taste the same.

They laugh.

Zenobia (*to Malik*) Give him wine.

Longinus (*hastily*) Thank you, no. (*to Wahballat*) You have before you a treatise on the art of excellence in literary composition. Literary composition is the highest achievement of the mortal mind, you know.

Wahballat Is it?

Zenobia (*aside to Malik*) What do you think?

Malik Harmless.

Zenobia Then he can stay. My son is happy, look at him. Is Zabdas at the palace?

Malik He's outside, buffing up his armour.

Zenobia Send him in.

Malik and the Guard exit.

Longinus, what is your attitude to Rome?

Longinus Rome is the sea. We are the waves.

Zenobia . . . You answer cautiously.

Longinus This is a Roman province, I believe?

17

Zenobia Can the sum of the waves ever be greater than the sea itself?

Longinus One has not studied the ocean, Majesty, or examined the virtues of its constituent parts.

Zenobia But is it possible the sea could split in two?

Longinus The Jews would have us believe so.

Zenobia Then you say it is possible.

Longinus I say there is textual evidence in the history of Moses . . . but historians, you know . . . notoriously unreliable. It is a hypothesis.

Zenobia Might the sea wage war on itself? Hypothetically speaking?

Longinus Experience, which is not a thing I am particularly fond of, would suggest that the sea is constantly at war with itself. There are whirlpools, currents, racing tides . . . the thunder of surf on the rocks . . . the dead calm of illusory peace. I have no doubt, Majesty, that the ocean is a natural battle-zone. Indeed, on my way here I was sick as a pig.

Zenobia Thank you. One thing more. If this sea had drowned your lover, how would you take revenge?

Longinus (*laughs*) I would take ten million buckets and sling it off the edge of the world.

> *Zenobia and Wahballat laugh.* **Zabdas,** *the Commander-in-Chief, enters escorted by Malik. Malik resumes fanning the Queen.*

Zenobia Commander. I am sorry to have kept you waiting.

Zabdas I have infinite patience, Majesty. My condolences, on this hateful day.

Zenobia We are finished with sorrow. We are forging ahead. I would like to know the precise disposition of our armies.

Zabdas May I ask the purpose?

Zenobia . . . My husband called you the Good Soldier. 'When I need my orders obeyed,' he told me, 'I send Zabdas.' I hope I can count on your loyalty.

Zabdas Aye, you can.

Zenobia Come what may?

Zabdas I will serve the wife of Odainat to my final breath.

Zenobia You serve not his wife but his blood. The line of Odainat rests in this boy, and in his descendants, and his descendants' descendants. For them we must take action. Casual slaughter on our own soil must not go unpunished! We are fortunate to have with us a wise man, Longinus of Greece. I have sought his advice, and he counsels quick reprisals.

Longinus (*worried*) I don't think I actually –

Zenobia Our forces stand ready, and hot for revenge. The only decision remaining to be taken is – where? North into Persia, east into Parthia, south into Palestine? Prepare your report.

Zabdas We have just made peace, Majesty.

Zenobia And no doubt we shall do so again, Commander. When the gains made by my husband have been consolidated. The time is auspicious. We *must* expand. For our country and this boy!

> *Wahballat is engrossed in the manuscript, and is not listening.*

Zabdas (*bowing*) It will be an honour to lead to victory the armies of Palmyra.

19

Zenobia An honour, yes. But *mine*.

Zabdas Naturally yours. All glory is yours. I simply mean that when we fight it will be me commanding.

Zenobia You miss the point. I will command. And not from some hilltop, either.

Zabdas With respect, you cannot lead the troops. You are a woman.

Zenobia I am a warrior.

Zabdas No, the men will not accept you.

Zenobia I will inspire them.

Zabdas Look, it isn't –

Zenobia My sex is immaterial! There is nothing manly in the field of battle that I cannot equal! Or do you challenge me?

Zabdas I? Fight you? (*He laughs lightly.*) No.

Zenobia You're beginning to annoy me, Zabdas.

Zabdas Nothing could be further from my wishes.

Zenobia (*angrily*) I was born to this. I am descended from Ptolemy of Egypt. The dynasty of Cleopatra! And you tell me a female cannot do great things! (*to Malik*) Stop fanning. Never fan me again. Never let it seem that I am weak. Let the sun burn me and the wind chill me; I will harden myself.

She rips off her headscarf.

This is how I will face the enemy. I will put shame in their hearts. They will be beaten by a woman. (*She turns to leave, then turns back.*) I know where to strike. Egypt!

Zabdas Egypt? Unthinkable!

Zenobia Why?

Zabdas The Romans have a standing army there!

Zenobia And is this just? Have they the right? Have they legitimate title to the lush lands of the Nile? Or should we not reclaim the kingdom of my ancestors, for Wahballat and his sons?

Zenobia exits with Malik. Pause.

Longinus Egypt supplies one-third of the grain that Rome needs to feed itself. The Emperior Gallienus will take it as an act of sedition.

Zabdas Scared, Greek?

Longinus A nice quiet place to retire, I thought. A little light research in the morning, a rest in the afternoon. (*He sighs.*)

Zabdas The Queen says you suggested this.

Longinus People *will* ask questions. One can but say what one thinks.

Zabdas Not in my profession.

Longinus Do you imply that a soldier never says what he thinks, or says what he doesn't think, or simply cannot think at all?

Zabdas exits angrily.

Wahballat (*looking up*) This is jolly interesting, Longinus. (*reads*) 'The greatest of all blessings is good fortune, and next to it comes good counsel, which, however, is no less important, since its absence leads to the complete destruction of what good fortune brings.' I'd never thought of that.

SCENE THREE

Palmyra. Three helmeted Soldiers enter fighting with swords, one against two. The **First Soldier** *defends well, until with a swirling slash the* **Third Soldier** *wounds the First Soldier, cutting him behind his knee. The First Soldier goes down in pain, blood flowing. They stop fighting immediately. The Third Soldier is Zenobia, dressed in full armour as a man. She throws down her sword, pulls off her helmet and turns to the* **Second Soldier**.

Zenobia Fetch help!

> *The Second Soldier leaves at a run. Zenobia kneels by the wounded First Soldier and pulls off his helmet. It is Zabdas.*

Zabdas, forgive me.

Zabdas I do.

Zenobia I was wild! I did not mean to hurt you!

Zabdas You have not hurt me.

Zenobia But – your leg –

Zabdas This meat is yours, to do with as you will. I bleed, but there is no pain.

Zenobia I tried to parry, but I was wild!

Zabdas A soldier must learn to control his passion.

Zenobia I will learn.

Zabdas Turn it on the enemy. Never on your friends.

Zenobia (*taking his head in her hands*) Never again, I swear to you!

Zabdas (*twisting his head away, as if in pain*) Majesty, you cannot be seen here. The people are not ready – a

22

woman in armour – there will be uproar. Go inside.

Zenobia And leave you wounded in the road?

Zabdas They will come for me. Go, I beg you.

Porphyry, *a student from Athens, enters and watches from a distance.*

Zenobia When may I be seen?

Zabdas What, as a man?

Zenobia No, simply as I wish to be.

Zabdas How is that?

Zenobia Simply free to act as I choose. Free not to be gentle, or kind. Free to fight! *When?*

Zabdas In the chaos of war, when all formality's abandoned, and the only law is the strength of your arm. Then you may cut hamstrings to your heart's content, but now, please – go!

Zenobia exits.

Aagh! The pain! Where she touched my face! Delicious pain! Her fingers, like snowflakes on my skin! She could slice every cord in my body, for one more touch of those hands!

Porphyry approaches Zabdas, who doesn't see him at first.

I never thought to be so close to heaven!

Porphyry What is it? Can I help you?

Zabdas How can you help me? You, a boy? You do not know the vicious thrust of love!

Porphyry (*kneeling*) Let me see.

Zabdas It is nothing. A scratch. A pleasure!

Porphyry You will bleed to death from this pleasure.

Porphyry takes the rope belt from around his waist and applies a tourniquet to Zabdas's thigh.

I have read that the flow of blood can be obstructed, if this is tight enough – there! I think we have staunched it. How did it happen?

Zabdas I dropped my guard. For a second, I dropped my guard. And the bright sharp blade drove in.

Soldiers run on, with a litter.

Soldier Over here!

Porphyry (*taking herbs from his shoulder-bag*) Apply these herbs to the wound, with balsam, if you can get it.

Zabdas . . . You are a capable lad. Where do you live? I'll reward you.

Porphyry I don't know, sir. It's my first day in Palmyra. I've got to find my master.

The Soldiers lift Zabdas on to the litter.

Soldier Easy now, Commander.

Zabdas You heard me cry out, didn't you?

Porphyry Yes, sir, as anyone would.

Zabdas Just pain, that's all, just agony –

Porphyry That's all I heard.

Zabdas Good boy. I'll remember you.

The Soldiers carry off Zabdas.

Porphyry What kind of place is this? The architecture of your dreams, and generals cut down in the streets? There are marble columns on every house, triumphal arches, treasure vaults, masonry wrought like filigree rings . . . And everywhere soldiers. Marching, drilling, racing dusty chariots through crowded alleys . . . The city smells of war.

Wahballat enters, reading as he walks.

Excuse me, I'm a stranger here. Can you tell me – the military activity? Is there going to be a battle?

Wahballat (*looks up from his page gloomily*) Several, I expect. (*He turns back to his manuscript and walks on.*)

Porphyry And what is the cause?

Wahballat My mother.

Porphyry laughs.

Oh, you think it's a joke? Perhaps you haven't got a mother? Mothers always know what's best for their children. You can try saying 'Mother, I actually have no need of half the world, I'm quite content at home,' but all you get is a withering look and a smart new uniform to wear. 'I'm doing all this for you,' they say. 'When you are older you will thank me.' There is nothing so ambitious as a mother.

Porphyry Mine was never ambitious for me. I had to strike out on my own.

Wahballat What are you, a lawyer?

Porphyry A philosopher.

Wahballat Gosh, that's what I want to be!

Porphyry (*abashed*) Well, I'm training.

Wahballat Ethics?

Porphyry Natural science.

25

Wahballat It's a long, hard road, isn't it? (*sighs, indicating his manuscript*) Been on the same page for a week.

Porphyry What's the text?

Wahballat It's new stuff. Pretty dense.

Porphyry May I? Hmm. (*reads*) 'No one would dispute that periphrasis contributes to the sublime. For as in music the sweetness of the dominant melody is enhanced by what are known as decorative additions, so periphrasis often harmonizes with the direct expression of a thought, and greatly embellishes it.' The style is familiar . . .

Wahballat Elegant speech is a terrible struggle.

Porphyry Personally I think it's over-rated, this fanatical obsession with oratory.

Wahballat Do you?

Porphyry Who needs to string fourteen sub-clauses and a pluperfect together, just to conduct an experiment? I incline to observation as the basis of all discovery.

Wahballat That's curious. My tutor says observation is the long holiday of the lazy thinker.

Porphyry Was he lying down when he said it?

Wahballat Come to think of it, he is fond of a snooze.

Porphyry Your tutor is – ?

Wahballat Cassius Longinus, of Athens.

Porphyry (*suddenly worried*) So you are – ?

Wahballat Me? Oh, I'm the King.

Porphyry throws himself to the ground in front of Wahballat.

Porphyry Majesty! I did not know.

Wahballat Perfectly all right. Don't get much conversation around here. It's a muscle-builder's paradise. A javelin-thrower's dream.

Porphyry I have brought the books.

Wahballat The books?

Porphyry My master's library, from Athens.

Wahballat You are Longinus's pupil? Oh, stand up, please. I'm so very happy to meet you. My name is Wahballat. You are called – ?

Porphyry Porphyry.

Wahballat And you are a scientist?

Porphyry Chemistry, mainly. My master disapproves. But it's the future, you see? It's the future!

Wahballat (*overjoyed*) Two schools of thought! Two! In Palmyra! Where before there was barely a glimmer! You are welcome, sir!

Porphyry It's a magnificent city.

Wahballat Yes, a magnificent city, somewhere on the outer rim of the cosmos. Tell me about the West. Is it true that you can buy –

Porphyry Majesty, I should find Longinus and unpack the books from the donkeys.

Wahballat Of course.

Porphyry You won't mention what I said . . . ? About the sub-clauses and so on?

Wahballat I heard nothing but enthusiasm. Come, I will take you to the palace.

Wahballat starts to lead Porphyry off.

Would you do something for me?

Porphyry (*smiles*) Anything you ask.

Wahballat Teach me, in secret. The rudiments of chemistry.

Porphyry It's a bit hit-and-miss –

Wahballat It's got to be better than playing at soldiers.

They laugh. As they exit, the sounds of a marching troop of infantry are heard off, growing ever louder until they merge into the noise of a great battle, from which emerges:

SCENE FOUR

Egypt. Zenobia alone on the battlefield, clad in a man's armour, but without a helmet. She carries a sword, literally dripping blood.

Zenobia It took all day. Hours and hours of killing. Pyramids of death. Now I know why they like it so much: the sheer exhilaration of being left alive at the end. Ankle-deep in offal, lips blistered from the sun, and a strange new taste in your mouth – (*She puts the bloody sword to her lips.*) – but still alive. There's no great mystery: you throw your weight through your shoulder, and swing. Sparks decorate your shield. A shudder rocks your arm as you strike the bone. A man's eyes glitter in your face, then fade. You step over his corpse, and go on. Always forward. Never back. Never look down at the face in the sand. The screams of the dead are like music.

My first battle. Now I am blooded. Now I know why they like it so much.

Rome. Two Senators, **Gratus** *and* **Quintinius**, *holding garlands of flowers.*

Quintinius They say she gives no quarter, but flails about like a dervish, her hair matted with blood, her sweating thighs quite naked; and hardened veterans of our Egyptian legions, facing this vision of unfeminine destruction, took to their heels and ran. They say she cut the beating heart from a man, and held it to her lips.

Gratus I once saw a Gaul do that in the arena. The audience were so impressed they yelled for more. So a Greek cut the heart from the Gaul.

Quintinius But they were men!

Gratus Absolutely, yes, I grant there is a difference. Do you see him yet?

Quintinius No.

Gratus He must pass this way to enter the Senate.

Quintinius With Egypt fallen, we will go short of bread. If the people lack bread, they will riot. Rome itself will resemble a battlefield.

Gratus And will subsequently need to be rebuilt, providing thereby a welcome fillip for the construction trade.

Quintinius (*grins*) I didn't get where I am today by not taking my opportunities.

Gratus Neatly put. No more did I. But it grieves me, this abysmal deterioration of public morals. In the golden days of the Republic, people would have begged to go hungry, and reached for their swords. Now we live in an age of baseness and dishonour.

Quintinius Do you suppose the new Emperor will have any noticeable effect?

Gratus In the immortal words of Tacitus, 'I hope for good Emperors, but I take them as they come.'

They laugh quietly. This conversation is discreet.

Yet another soldier, I gather?

Quintinius Cavalry man. Risen from the ranks. Son of a Pannonian peasant.

Gratus My point exactly. Standards have declined. We are ruled by the dregs of the Danube.

Quintinius Already I miss Gallienus.

Gratus Yes, he may have had the shortest reign in history, but he knew how to put on a show.

Quintinius He certainly did. And the spectacles you staged for him were beyond compare. The naval battle on the artificial lake . . . I'll never forget that . . .

Gratus Four thousand drowned. Went like a dream.

Quintinius Good old Gallienus.

Gratus He spent public money with a vengeance, the fat bastard.

Quintinius And what did it get him?

Gratus A knife in the guts.

They laugh quietly.

Quintinius . . . Here comes his successor. A crate of oysters says he doesn't live five years.

Gratus Done.

*The Emperor **Aurelian** enters with his Tribune, **Probus**,*

and a squad of Soldiers guarding him closely. The
Senators bow and offer their garlands.

A warm welcome to Rome, stern victor of the North. The
Senate salutes you. Jupiter, Juno and Minerva smile down
on you. And honest citizens sleep safely in their beds, now
the German menace has been checked.

Aurelian stays tight behind his bodyguard. He nods to
Probus, who takes the garlands.

Probus I accept them on the Emperor's behalf. Your
name?

Gratus Septimus Gratus.

Quintinius Lollius Quintinius.

Probus Thank you, Senators.

Aurelian nods to the Senators, and the squad begins to
march on.

Quintinius Emperor . . . the revolt in the East?

Aurelian stops.

Gratus The woman who fights like a man . . . ?

Quintinius What measures have you taken?

Gratus When will you be marching out again?

Aurelian nods to Probus.

Probus We do not perceive the threat to be sufficiently
volatile to justify an armed response.

Quintinius But she has taken Egypt!

Probus And she will hand it back. We have sued for
peace.

Quintinius Peace!

Probus The Palmyrenes are merchants. They will deal. The wheatfields of Egypt are a bargaining tool. There is no direct challenge to Imperial rule.

Gratus With the greatest respect, Emperor, the Senate will never permit you to negotiate with barbarians.

Probus It is done already. Envoys have been sent.

Gratus But this is an outrage! Held to ransom? By a woman?

Aurelian (*losing patience*) Look. I fuck women. I don't fight them. My men would laugh at me.

Quintinius But we have not debated it!

Aurelian shrugs.

We have protocols, traditions . . .

Aurelian Good for you.

Aurelian walks on. Gratus goes after him.

Gratus Emperor, I feel sure we can come rapidly to a consensus on foreign policy, but there is also the outstanding matter of the Roman Mint – which you have closed down –

Aurelian ignores him and exits with the Soldiers.

Probus The coinage is debased. Tin passing for silver. Chicanery and deceit. We are initiating a raft of currency reforms. Meanwhile the Mint remains closed.

Gratus Tribune, there is no problem with the currency; you've either got it or you haven't, that's the meat of the matter. Really, no cause to be extreme. We simply need to sit down together and thrash this out, over a glass or two. Would you be so good as to invite the Emperor to come to dinner, at my villa in Tivoli?

Probus The Emperor doesn't eat dinner.

Probus exits.

Gratus Pannonian arsehole! What did we do to deserve
him?

Quintinius We sold our souls to the army. To keep the
wild wolf from the door.

Gratus And now they think they can govern by
themselves!

Quintinius (*sighs*) Bring back the old days.

Gratus Yes, absolutely, bring back Gallienus! At least he
liked his food.

SCENE SIX

*Palmyra. A private room in the palace. Zenobia enters in
full armour, dusty and exhausted. Malik follows. Piece by
piece he removes her armour.*

Malik You should have ridden back from Egypt. In a
chariot. Or on a horse.

Zenobia I wanted to walk with my men. We sang songs of
victory, all the way home. At night we drank by camp-fires
and compared our looted treasure. Never have I felt more
alive.

Malik I'm delighted for you, Majesty. Sadly your
shoulders somehow failed to get the message. They are
crabbed like an old, stunted vine.

Zenobia I carried my sword and my pack.

Malik (*groans*) But you are Queen!

Zenobia They must never see me weaken. One slip, and I
am gone.

33

Malik laughs to himself.

Are you laughing at me, Malik?

Malik No, at us. At the irony of it. I almost a woman. You almost a man.

Zenobia Would you like to be a woman?

Malik Ooh, yes please. Do you know a magic spell?

Zenobia What is it that appeals?

Malik You have things done to you. You do not have to *do* them.

Zenobia But I like to do things.

Malik You will tire of it, Majesty. Women are allowed to change their minds. And are wonderfully good at it, I believe.

Zenobia I hate women –

Malik No –

Zenobia – their flabby arms, their make-up, their smell of cooking oil –

Malik This is why you sent away your daughters?

Zenobia Girls are a distraction in a war.

Malik Yes, they were pretty.

Zenobia No they weren't. They were just weak. Do something to my back, please.

Zenobia lies down and Malik massages her back.

Higher . . . higher . . . there. Aah . . . The Romans have offered us peace.

Malik Sweet of them.

34

Zenobia In return for abandoning Egypt, they will give us the right to crown Wahballat Emperor of the East – or, as the document puts it, 'Imperator Caesar Julius Aurelius Septimius Vaballathus, Persicus Maximus, Arabicus Maximus, the Devout, the Fortunate, the Unconquered, Augustus'.

Malik Some scribe with a sense of history, killing the hours till lunchtime . . . And yourself, Majesty?

Zenobia Me? I am nothing. Me they do not recognize.

Malik I have never met a Roman who was not a ghastly snob.

Zenobia I don't know what to do.

Malik Anything Roman is always better than anything else. They go somewhere foreign, and want to make it just like home. They want the same food, the same entertainment, the same over-heated rooms – see them cruising the bazaars in their ghastly clothes, talking loudly in Latin, as if mere noise will make them understood – haggling for trinkets that look 'typically ethnic' – all the time assuming that their money buys respect. Total world domination is a hideous thing.

Zenobia What shall I do?

Malik And their sense of geography! A Roman once asked if I had relatives in India! He thought it was just down the road!

Zenobia Malik, I don't know what to do! The troops are exultant. They would fight for a field of stones. I have only to say 'advance'. We could take Mesopotamia, Persia – we could blaze to the shores of Byzantium, and have Europe at our feet!

Malik So what's stopping you?

Zenobia There is a new Emperor.

Malik They do like a change, don't they?

Zenobia He is called Aurelian. My intelligence says he is not like the others. He can fight. He rules his army with a fist of iron. He has secured the northern border, leaving villages burning in the forests, men impaled on trees. He is not the kind of soft fruit we are used to. He is hard. I dream of him, Malik. I conjure his face. I try to guess how he will act. I can lead us to the brink of all-out war – push at the skin of the Empire, and see if it will split – but how will he respond? Will he retaliate in numbers, or leave the East to us?

Malik What I know about military strategy you could carve on a grain of salt.

Zenobia I must know what he's thinking . . . !

Malik Well, take advice.

Zenobia From?

Malik Your advisors. All those clever fellows you employ.

Zenobia The only one I trust is you.

Malik But I'm the stupidest.

Zenobia You're my friend.

Malik Majesty, you have no friends. (*Beat.*) I am your slave. I love you as a slave.

She looks sad.

Do you remember, when first you were married, how I would entertain you?

Zenobia nods.

Relax. Clear your mind of everything.

Malik signals to some **Musicians***, who begin to play.
Then he dances – a sensuous, erotic dance – and sings:*

'A bed of flowers
A bed of straw
A bed of feathers
From African birds
A bath of milk
A scented garden
Or rolling, tumbling by
The waterside . . .

I will lie with you
Anywhere you choose.'

When he is finished:

Now – say quickly – what do you *want*?

Zenobia I want to carve a stronghold for my line of future kings. I want my son and his son's sons to reign with honour and pride, not as puppets of the West. I want the state of Palmyra to endure for ever, the greatest society the desert's ever known.

Malik And for yourself?

Zenobia I want Rome.

SCENE SEVEN

Wahballat's library. Longinus lies asleep on a couch, a book open on his chest. Nearby, Wahballat and Porphyry work on a secret chemical experiment with a makeshift apparatus. A glass alembic is heated over glowing embers from the fire. They speak softly, surrounded by huge, dusty books and phials of powder.

Porphyry I've extracted arsenic from realgar, and white

37

lead from litharge. But mercury from cinnabar defeats me.

Wahballat How do you go about it?

Porphyry A process of distillation, perfected in Alexandria a century ago. It's all there in the secret books.

Wahballat Why are they secret?

Porphyry Because if anyone found out what we were doing, they would think we were mad. The world is unaware of what is possible. People are suspicious. Does he still sleep?

Wahballat (*looking at Longinus*) Like a baby.

Porphyry Good. Now we can work. Read me that passage, please.

Wahballat (*consulting a book*) 'Neither plants, nor elements, nor stones are mature until the fire has tested them. When they are cloaked in splendour from the fire they will put on divers heavenly colours, and then will appear their hidden glory – their transformation to the divine state of fusion.' Who wrote this?

Porphyry A scientist, Mary the Jewess.

Wahballat A woman?

Porphyry A brave woman.

Wahballat What does it mean, Porphyry?

Porphyry It is the great poem of life.

Wahballat A poem? I thought we were off all that!

Porphyry (*smiles*) Nothing is what it seems, Majesty.

Wahballat Please, call me Wahballat.

Porphyry I am today attempting to distill the essence of nitre. Do you understand what nitre is?

Wahballat No, I don't. (*sighs*) I don't understand anything.

Porphyry shows him some nitre.

Pooh! It stinks.

Porphyry I get it from the camel stables. Some mystical reaction in the soil.

Wahballat It's camel shit?

Porphyry It was camel shit. Now it's a chemical element called salt of potassium.

Wahballat I say, this is jolly good fun!

Porphyry The earth reveals its secrets to the wise. You know the pigment they call 'imperial purple'? That dyes the Emperor's cloak?

Wahballat I know it costs a fortune.

Porphyry But where does it come from?

Wahballat shakes his head.

Shellfish.

Wahballat Shellfish?

Porphyry You farm it, a few drops at a time, from a gland in a species of mollusc found only in Phoenicia. (*with a glance at Longinus*) Try gleaning that from a well-turned peroration. But let us proceed with the experiment. This nitre is the agent. Blue vitriol – here – the reagent. I am adding some charcoal, for its combustible properties are well known. Gently heat. What forms in the collecting glass should be the essence.

Wahballat What can you do with this essence?

Porphyry It can separate silver from gold.

Wahballat Why would you wish to do that?

Porphyry Purity.

Wahballat You want pure gold?

Porphyry I want purity.

Wahballat You disappoint me. You are doing this just to get rich! I can make you rich, if that is your desire. But wealth alone is nothing. Knowledge is supreme. I thought you were an explorer, probing the recesses of nature.

Porphyry I am!

Wahballat I thought this was an odyssey of learning!

Porphyry It is!

Wahballat Look here, I know what you're up to – you're trying to make gold!

Porphyry I never said that!

  Longinus stirs. They quieten.

I am trying to make *medicine*. The properties of minerals are central to that pursuit. I am trying to find the drug that will cure all pain.

Wahballat Is there such a thing?

Porphyry The ancient masters thought so. There exists a universal spirit, I am sure of it. And all matter can be reduced to this chief agent, given skill and dedication. One day someone will discover the essential power that will heal wounds, retard decay, prolong your days indefinitely.

Wahballat Eternal youth?

Porphyry Why not?

Wahballat Tantalizing!

Porphyry Why must we age, and decline, and die? Once we understand the driving force of life, what benefits will follow?

Wahballat And you will do this! And I will be your apprentice!

Porphyry (*smiles*) Perhaps. There's the small problem of our acid of nitre, though, which as yet we have not solved. And it looks like the fire's going out.

   Wahballat takes a bellows to the fire.

Wahballat Awfully sorry I spoke so harshly. I jump to conclusions – forgive me. I would like to be your friend. There are so few people I can talk to.

Porphyry You are not like the others.

Wahballat Nor are you.

Porphyry How strange, that I should find my way to Syria, and you and I should meet.

Wahballat When we are together I –

Porphyry (*suddenly businesslike*) No activity in the alembic. I think sulphur should be added.

Wahballat Have you a reason?

Porphyry Oh, I add sulphur to everything, just like my mother added salt.

   Porphyry finds a phial of powdered sulphur and
   measures out a small quantity.

Wahballat . . . My mother never cooked. Or sewed. Or laundered shirts. I never saw her singing, like the women by the wells. Always regal, always riding with the men. I don't know what a normal home is.

Porphyry Nothing special.

Wahballat I wish my brother Hairan was alive. He didn't like me. But at least there'd be peace in Palmyra.

Porphyry tips the sulphur into the apparatus. The retort explodes with a loud bang. The apparatus is shattered, but no one is hurt. The noise wakes Longinus.

Longinus The five sources of sublimity!

As Longinus sits up, he drops to the floor the cochlis brooch he has hidden under his robe. Nobody notices this. Porphyry and Wahballat hastily hide their alchemical textbooks and the ruined apparatus, and pick up the work they ought to have been studying.

As I was saying, the five sources of sublimity *are* – ?

Porphyry The ability to form grand conceptions, master.

Wahballat The stimulus of powerful emotion –

Longinus – though some emotions are mean, and not in the least sublime –

Porphyry The proper formation of the two types of figure, namely, figures of thought and figures of speech –

Wahballat – coupled with the choice of words, the use of imagery and the elaboration of style.

Longinus The fifth source of grandeur embraces all those already mentioned, and it is the total effect resulting from dignity and elevation. What was that ghastly noise?

Wahballat (*to Porphyry*) Did you hear a noise?

Porphyry I was intent on my studies.

Wahballat I too. Perhaps you were dreaming, Longinus?

Longinus Dreaming, Majesty? (*It occurs to him that perhaps he was.*) An old affliction, nothing more. Wounds won in the cause of art. The crash of split infinitives, the hoot of rude tumidity, the bombast of the third-rate panegyrist – this clamour fills my head from time to time.

Wahballat I expect that was it, then.

Longinus We must strive to eliminate all ignoble forms, before we are deafened by inconcinnous debate. (*to Porphyry*) What is the text for today?

Porphyry Book Sixteen of the *Iliad,* master.

Longinus Well fetch it down, man, fetch it – this is no *experiment,* to sit and watch for hours – this is literature, literature fit for a King!

Porphyry climbs a ladder to reach the book.

Wahballat Let me help you. (*aside to Porphyry*) Well, that was jolly interesting, wasn't it?

Porphyry (*aside to Wahballat*) What on earth happened?

Longinus (*to himself*) Could have sworn I heard a bang . . .

Yedibel enters.

We are at our books, sir.

Yedibel Then you must put them away, Longinus. The Queen is coming.

Longinus (*jumps up*) The Queen? I am barely awake!

Yedibel The Queen has consulted the oracle of Aphrodite Aphacitis, as to whether the war should be prolonged. You are required to interpret the signs.

Yedibel exits. Wahballat and Porphyry come to Longinus with the Iliad.

Longinus Runes, entrails, chicken's blood – what signs? Interpret – advise – oh, heaven! The Queen – courtiers – any minute!

Wahballat Asyndeton, or the omission of conjunctions?

Longinus Quite correct. To give the impression of agitation. Porphyry, bring everything we've got on prediction. Quick! Never done oracles before. Witness the final humiliation of logic, in a welter of omens and spells!

> *Porphyry runs to fetch the books. Zenobia enters with Zabdas, dragging his bad leg, Timagenes, Yedibel, Malik and other Courtiers. Zenobia wears a customized version of her army uniform: a short tunic, with gems dangling from its lower edge. Her arms and legs are bare, and a short sword hangs at her side. Malik carries a tray bearing the sacred offerings.*

Most illustrious exarch of the Palmyrenes, welcome to our cave of mental labour. The great library is complete!

Wahballat Absolutely first-class tuition, mother, without a doubt.

Zenobia You would not have thanked me had I brought you a charlatan. Longinus, we need your help. Some of us believe we should reject the Romans' overtures of peace, and challenge their authority throughout the whole of Asia. Some others of us feel differently, asserting that peace will benefit trade, that we have all the wealth we need, and that the terms from Rome are in fact quite favourable.

Zabdas Favourable? We beat them!

Timagenes But why waste more life? It will all end in destruction.

Zenobia As you see we are divided. So I made a pilgrimage to Heliopolis. I sacrificed at the shrine of Aphrodite, and offered my gifts to the sacred pool. As I did so I asked for advice.

Porphyry places open volumes before Longinus, and indicates sections of text.

Porphyry Here, here, and here.

Zenobia Into the pool I placed gold, silver, linen and silk, consecrated by the Priestess of the temple, and blessed by every church.

Longinus (*reading fast*) They sank to the bottom?

Zenobia Yes.

Longinus Good.

Zenobia Then they rose back to the top.

Longinus Ah.

Zenobia What are we to make of this?

Timagenes A bad augury, is it not, philosopher? A sign that further war will court disaster?

Zenobia Or a miracle, perhaps? A thing of joy?

Longinus If I might have a moment or two for consultation – ?

Zabdas Get on with it, Greek. Thirty thousand archers stand at arms.

Longinus (*aside to Porphyry*) I think we could call this a conundrum.

Porphyry (*aside to Longinus*) She likes to fight.

Longinus (*aside*) What?

Porphyry (*aside*) Be careful, master.

Longinus . . . Majesty, albeit the weapons of divination and clairvoyance have no true rank in the rhetorician's arsenal, I will venture a gloss on the preternatural wonders

45

you have seen. Gold, silver, linen and silk are representative of all your prosperity on earth. By casting them into the sacred pool, you demonstrate your willingness to renounce them. What is the official state religion?

Zenobia We have none. All faiths are accommodated, from Jews to votaries of the Sun.

Yedibel We even have a Christian, Paul of Samosata.

Longinus An enlightened policy. And you are right. It is all one. All roads lead to the centre. We serve a Great Unknown, a Demiurge, creator of the Universal Mind.

Zabdas Cut the riddles. Speak to the point.

Longinus The point? We are dealing with a celestial allegory, Commander. The divine riddle of the future. One is not convinced there is a *point*.

Longinus turns to Porphyry, who whispers in his ear.

The gifts rose back to the surface. Did they float?

Zenobia Yes.

Longinus Defiant of physical laws! Then what happened?

Zenobia The Priestess made us take them away. Now we don't know what to do with them.

Longinus Treasure them! Encase them in your deepest vaults! They have been sanctioned by heaven! The gods have viewed your worldly goods, and sent them back to you, imbued with esoteric properties. They approve your actions.

Zenobia In taking Egypt?

Longinus In taking Egypt, Majesty, and, I think, in defying Rome. The connotation is clear. If you risk your most precious assets, they shall return to you, with even greater value than before. Whatever you choose is for the best.

Timagenes Bah! Longinus, you preposterous sycophant!

Longinus You doubt the omniscience of the oracle?

Timagenes The gifts are meant to vanish in the depths of the pool – any fool knows that!

Longinus Queen Zenobia has not been answered in the standard way, with that I can concur. And why not? Because she has not inconvenienced the deities with the standard problems: will I become rich? can my foot-rot be cured? is my wife in bed with the taxman? No, the Queen has posed the question of a great and zealous nation. Its heritage. Its destiny. I am not surprised, not in the least, that Aphrodite smiled.

Zenobia Then we should pursue a course of war?

Longinus I don't think I said that, did I?

Zabdas (*to Zenobia*) But what you choose is for the best. He said *that*. Clear as a bell.

Timagenes I cannot believe you are taken in like this, Majesty!

Zenobia Timagenes suggests my judgement is unsound.

Timagenes No, but you fight out of pride!

Zenobia Pride? Yes. That's why I fight. And have you none? No feeling for your country?

Timagenes I am First Minister. Head of all the Tribes. I care for the land, for the people. Of course I am proud; but proud of our intelligence, our statesmanship, our will to survive!

Zenobia Like fleas in the fur of our oppressors. Is how we survive.

Wahballat I say, that's a bit rich –

Zenobia Be quiet. I have a vision of the future. We are making Palmyra an oasis not of wells and springs, but of culture, of science, of tolerance and achievement. Longinus has spoken well; and Timagenes has strengthened my resolve, with his fears and his appeasements, like a rat scuttling for cover when the sandstorm blows up.

Timagenes May I remind you of my position –

Zenobia You have no position! Kneel!

Reluctantly, Timagenes kneels. Zenobia draws her sword and holds it to his neck. The Courtiers pull back.

I swing my arm. That's all. What can you say to save your life?

Timagenes No – no –

Zenobia Is he eloquent in his plea, Longinus? You judge.

Longinus Me?

Wahballat (*to Zenobia*) You are making yourself look ridiculous!

Zenobia Ruthlessness is not thought ridiculous in a man. (*to Timagenes*) You oppose me. Why should I not cut your head off?

Timagenes I don't want to die!

Longinus A line of high poetry, Majesty, in my opinion . . .

Zenobia I have read Homer. That was not poetry.

Longinus It had a sincerity – a naïve charm –

Zenobia Metre? Assonance?

Longinus But the sentiments expressed – a universal truth –

Zenobia But so unoriginal!

Zenobia swings her arm.

Wahballat Mother! I thought we were going to be tolerant!

Zenobia lowers her sword, glaring at him.

Zenobia So we were. (*to* Timagenes) Get out. I strip you of your office.

Timagenes Thank you, Majesty.

Zenobia Thank literary criticism. Not previously known for its valour.

Timagenes bows to Longinus and Wahballat and exits.

Yedibel.

Yedibel Majesty?

Zenobia Your views on the war?

Yedibel The heroic struggle of a downtrodden people against imperialism and servitude, Majesty.

Zenobia I appoint you First Minister. (*to* Longinus) Once more we are grateful to you for your guidance. Please accompany us to the Temple of Bel, where we shall put the holy relics on display.

Zenobia, Malik, Longinus, Zabdas, Yedibel and the Courtiers exit. Wahballat lags behind to be near Porphyry, who is putting the books away.

Wahballat What caused that explosion, do you suppose?

Porphyry Let's just say I don't think the five sources of sublimity had a great deal to do with it. But maybe the sulphur . . .

Zabdas returns.

Zabdas Majesty, your mother requests your presence at the Temple, in a certain tone of voice we both know well. I should hurry along if I were you.

Wahballat (*sighs*) Oh, public duties, such a bore. Until tomorrow, then, Porphyry?

Porphyry Tomorrow, Wahballat.

Wahballat leaves.

Zabdas You are too familiar with the monarch. He is an innocent. Do not lead him astray.

Porphyry I am young, too.

Zabdas (*laughs*) You know more than you let on. A good quality. And if I am not mistaken, we may count deciphering the signs among your talents.

Porphyry Everything I know is learnt from my master.

Zabdas Oh aye, I'm sure.

Porphyry I think you got what you want.

Zabdas What the Queen wants . . . is what I want.

Porphyry How is your leg?

Zabdas I can't fight. But I can walk. Thanks to you.

Porphyry And . . . how is your heart, Commander?

Zabdas You are good with secrets, aren't you, boy? (*He hesitates, but:*) King Odainat and I were from the same tribe. Friends since boyhood. But the day he married for the second time, something died between us. Because I wanted his wife. I gave my life to the service of my friend. In order to be near *her*. And then, one day – pff! – he is gone. And I have not the courage to act. Fine soldier, me. Is there anything . . . you could do for my condition?

Porphyry You mean – a magic potion? Slip it in her drink?

Zabdas Aye. Turn her gaze towards me.

Porphyry Do you think I am a sorcerer?

Zabdas I have seen you in the camel sheds, raking through the muck. I have seen you with a candle in the middle of the night, delving into dark, forbidden books. I know you have powers not given to most men. Help me.

Porphyry I know nothing of love.

Zabdas Just get her to notice me once in a while!

Porphyry I can give you no potion, for none exists. But may I give you some advice? Don't do as she wants.

Zabdas What?

Porphyry Contradict her.

Zabdas Are you daft?

Porphyry Be difficult. Be prickly. Show her your mind is your own.

Zabdas All my life I have learnt to obey. Now I should be insubordinate?

Porphyry Yes. Leave a little ripple on the water.

Zabdas How do you know this will work?

Porphyry I don't. I've never tried to seduce a Queen.

Zabdas finds on the floor the cochlis brooch dropped by Longinus.

Zabdas Is this yours?

Porphyry No, sir.

Zabdas Your master's?

Porphyry (*shakes his head*) My master scorns all possessions.

Zabdas Strange. I feel like I've seen it before. (*He pockets it.*) I will try your advice. It has merit.

Porphyry Good luck, Commander. In love and war.

SCENE EIGHT

Rome. A military map-room. Aurelian is tossing a coin. He is with **Pertinax,** *a* **Prefect,** *and a* **General.**

Pertinax All the lands of the East have fallen to Zenobia. Three legions have been lost: the Third Gallica, the Fourth Scythica, and the Sixteenth Flavia Firma. She swept them away like the autumn leaves.

Aurelian What, with a handful of brigands?

Pertinax The Bedouin cavalry are fierce opponents, Emperor.

Aurelian A bunch of cunts on camels. With knives between their teeth.

Prefect Still, they control Asia Minor.

Aurelian Not for long.

Probus enters.

Probus. Take a look at this.

Aurelian flips him the coin.

Probus Syrian currency?

Aurelian The other side.

Probus (*turning the coin over*) Bloody cheek.

Aurelian She has proclaimed herself Empress. Her face on my coin! And her brat she calls 'Augustus'.

Probus Where did it come from?

Pertinax The Mint at Antioch.

Aurelian The Mint at Alexandria is also in her hands. So we can kiss goodbye to fiscal reforms. If any fucking Arab can make money, what's the point of curbing the issue at home? We might as well use pebbles from the street! Inflation will soar! And all those bent Senators will snigger in their sleeves.

Probus You can't let a woman do this to you.

Aurelian (*spits*) I know that.

Prefect So what do you propose?

Aurelian Tie the bitch's legs to elephants' tails, and split her like a rabbit for the pot.

Probus I take it the time for diplomacy is past?

Aurelian I should learn to stick to what I'm good at. Pertinax – how long to march to this desert?

Pertinax We calculate a hundred and twenty days.

Probus Emperor, you are used to fighting in the bogs and forests, where water is plentiful and cover secure. This terrain is very different.

Aurelian I will adapt.

General Even the maps are guesswork!

Aurelian There is no choice! What am I supposed to do, let some perfumed nomad take a third of the Empire and shove it up my arse? Without the provinces we are nothing; Rome is just a vessel, into which their products pour. Gold from Spain, tin from Britain, amber from the Baltic – how could we live without any of this? The Empire *is* the world. I will not see it fracture. Nor can I tackle our domestic problems, until the frontiers are secure. That (*the coin*) is an act of rebellion. (*to Pertinax*) Set the wheels in motion.

Pertinax How many legions?

Aurelian We must leave sufficient troops on the Rhine and the Danube, and for the defence of Rome. We will draw upon our allies in the East. Say, six legions plus auxiliaries.

Prefect Forty thousand men.

Probus The Palmyrenes have seventy thousand.

Aurelian Yes, but I'm talking about soldiers.

Prefect One trained Roman's worth two sun-worshippers any day of the week.

Pertinax The supply line's going to be our biggest headache.

General That and the Persian clap.

Pertinax Siege machinery?

Aurelian Yes.

Probus You're going to haul catapults through the mountains of Cilicia?

Aurelian With my teeth if necessary. To your business, gentlemen.

Pertinax Emperor, we salute you.

Pertinax exits with the officers.

Aurelian . . . I feel better. This is what I know.

Probus You're going to war against a female.

Aurelian It's not just her on her own . . . !

Probus It is not honourable. It is tinged with shame.

Aurelian *Losing* is dishonour. I don't intend to lose.

Probus And when you win, what will you do with her?

Aurelian . . . I'm fucked if I know.

SCENE NINE

Palmyra. Zenobia's palace. She and Wahballat are on a balcony, facing upstage, taking the salute from a march-past of soldiers and a cheering crowd. Wahballat now wears robes of imperial purple, a garland on his head. Zenobia has purple swatches attached to her army uniform. Malik waits within. As the cheering continues, Zenobia and Wahballat acknowledge it with one last wave and come inside. Malik approaches with a tray of drinks.

Wahballat This adulation is exhausting. I'm completely fagged.

Zenobia The spontaneous joy of the people cannot lightly be dismissed. I love this city, look at it. The evening sunlight playing on the avenues of stone . . . ! Isn't it wonderful, what we've built?

Wahballat You did it, Mother. Not I. You have created your utopia. Poets and thinkers flock here like migrating birds.

Zenobia Strange, though, how when you've achieved what you most desired, it does not satisfy.

Wahballat What do you mean?

Zenobia Nothing. But I never have time to read the books. They all seem so irrelevant.

Wahballat One day books will be written about you. I daresay then you'll read them.

Zenobia I will presumably be dead. (*She has an idea.*) Malik, fetch the philosopher.

Malik exits. Outside, the people cheer.

Listen. The crime of the Romans has been answered. And they have no riposte. They are silent! Now *we* are the noise at the centre of things. We pulse with collective energy, the envy of the world. But you look glum. Why are you glum? You always sulk at parties.

Wahballat I spend so much time as the figurehead of the nation . . . I am way behind with my work.

Zenobia You would rather be in some dusty study, than living the life of a god?

Wahballat Well, yes, actually.

Zenobia What's so attractive about it?

Wahballat Oh, nothing. The company of friends.

Zenobia . . . Wait a minute. You have gone soft on the Greek boy.

Wahballat We get on awfully well, do you see –

Zenobia Are you sleeping with him?

Wahballat I don't know what you're talking about, mother.

Zenobia It wouldn't surprise me . . . the Greeks are famous for it.

Wahballat Look here, we're just jolly good friends!

Zenobia Yet you find him attractive –

Wahballat I do, yes, I do –

Zenobia A man loves women. Do you want to be a man?

Wahballat I was rather hoping to avoid the issue –

Zenobia What?

Wahballat – until I've made my mind up.

   Pause.

Zenobia Malik castrated himself when he was twelve.

Wahballat Goodness me! Why?

Zenobia For a job in the royal household. Is that how you wish to be? Like him? (*She draws her sword and offers it to him.*) Here.

Wahballat Now let's not get over-dramatic –

Zenobia If you're only half a man, dispose of the bits you don't need.

Wahballat I told you, I'm undecided!

Zenobia I cannot abide indecision!

Wahballat Well, I'm not chopping my thing off just to make you feel better!

Zenobia All right, I'll do it for you.

Wahballat No!

   She pursues him with the sword. Malik and Longinus enter.

Longinus You wished to see me, Majesty?

Zenobia I have a commission for you. The History of the Palmyrene Wars.

Longinus They are over?

Wahballat (*gloomily*) We won.

Zenobia I want a comprehensive record, in the epic style, of all our gains and conquests. With descriptions of the battles. And the heroes of the day.

Longinus I am to write this?

Zenobia Yes, you, the Sublime Longinus, in your inimitable syntax.

Longinus One is not sure one has the sensibilities of an historian, Majesty.

Zenobia Then apply the sensibilities of the poet. Elaborate. Apostrophize.

Wahballat Periphrasis, Longinus.

Longinus I know what it is, thank you.

Zenobia Include also the wondrous intellectual melting-pot our city has become. We have such personalities dwelling among us! Callinicus of Petra, Nicomachus of Trebizond –

Wahballat – all brought here by the lure of Arab gold.

Zenobia You have parchment? You have ink?

Longinus Plenty of ink.

Zenobia Then begin.

Longinus With the greatest respect, I – (*realizing he has no choice*) Where would be the most appropriate starting point? The hour of your Majesty's birth?

Yedibel enters in a hurry, with a dirty, exhausted
Bedouin Scout.

Zenobia Minister? You were not announced.

Yedibel I bring bad news – a Roman army has crossed the
Bosphorous! They advance southwards at a feverish pace!

Zenobia Are you sure?

Yedibel This scout rode day and night to warn us!

Scout Three camels died under me. I have not slept for a
week. They march like devils! Never eat, never drink! At
night each soldier takes a shovel and fortifies the camp – a
city springs up in the desert, ringed around with stakes!
They are not just Romans, but a western coalition – as
well as the Gothic legions, the Dalmatian cavalry, and the
Moesians and Pannonians, they have Celts, Britons,
Spaniards – and they bring siege engines! Huge
instruments of war! Ballistas, catapults, battering-rams!
And the Emperor Aurelian is riding at their head!

Zenobia . . . So he is coming. Good. The final test. The
reckoning.

She exchanges a look with Malik.

Yedibel, conscript ten thousand men, and begin the
building of a wall.

Yedibel A wall, Majesty?

Zenobia A wall around the city. Four storeys high, with
towers, checkpoints, sally-ports. An insurmountable wall.
I must alert Zabdas.

Longinus Would it perhaps be wise to delay the
commencement of what I have provisionally entitled *The
Chronicles of Zenobia* until we have tried conclusions
with the Romans, Majesty?

Zenobia No. You will march with us, to report at first-hand on the death-throes of an Empire. You will stand in the front line of history, and trumpet the cause of the East!

Zenobia exits, with Malik, Yedibel and the Scout. Longinus is dismayed.

Wahballat You see? All the big celebrities eventually come to Palmyra. Now we've hooked Aurelian, the most powerful man in the world.

Longinus The *front line* . . . ?

Wahballat Another great honour, Longinus. Soon you will be winning medals.

Longinus I'm a *philosopher*!

Wahballat You're a slave, old man. A hired mind. I take it Porphyry will remain behind, to continue my tutorials?

Longinus Porphyry? No, I need him! For the book!

Wahballat I need him.

Longinus You think I can write it on my own?

Wahballat I need him. That is an imperial command. You may go.

Longinus Oh, if I could find my brooch . . .

Longinus bows and exits.

Wahballat I need him . . . like the cactus needs a single drop of rain . . . to yield a gorgeous flower.

Timagenes enters, furtively.

Timagenes Emperor, I beg an audience. I have been ostracized. I am a jackal, on the fringe of society. And why? Because I plead for peace. The people have dust in their eyes! Your mother is a tyrant.

Wahballat Now steady on, Timagenes, that's a bit steep.

Timagenes She would have me killed if she saw me here. But you are not so cruel. You are not a warmonger. The dragon-banners and battle-rites have no place in your heart. You are a man of moderation. Wahballat, it is time to oppose belligerence and hate! These Romans are connoisseurs of death. They will break us, crush us in their fingernails like so many lice – mounds of corpses will line the colonnades – the courtyards of the palace will run with Arab blood! We can stop this!

Wahballat How?

Timagenes Overthrow the Queen.

Wahballat Oh dear.

Timagenes The priests of the temples are with me – several of the tribal chiefs – a caucus in the Senate. Join us. (*He hears someone approaching.*) Think hard! You could prevent a slaughter!

Timagenes exits as Malik enters.

Wahballat Oh dear, dear, dear . . .

Malik Emperor, a council of war has been summoned. You must take your seat at the head of the table. Zabdas has a strategy – to allow the invaders deep into our land, and confront them in the harshness of the desert, which we know well – and where they will die like dogs, he says.

Wahballat And what do you think? How do the Romans look?

Malik Oh, the Praetorian Guard have a dazzling uniform, apparently.

Wahballat Malik . . . Tell me what it's like to love a man.

Malik Majesty, it is no different from any other kind of loving. But I will tell you what I know.

SCENE TEN

The Roman lines at Emesa, in the desert. Night. Torches blazing. Standards stuck in the ground. Aurelian and Probus, wrapped up against the cold. Dogs and horses in the distance.

Probus I don't understand why they've let us come this far. We were not harried in the mountains; the passes of Cilicia lay open and unguarded. And now, suddenly, they are here. I can see the flicker of their fires.

Aurelian She is cunning. She knows her strength is in her mounted regiments. So they have drawn us on to open ground. It won't make any difference.

Probus We're outnumbered nearly two to one, Emperor.

Aurelian But we have something they lack. Discipline. What is that town behind their lines?

Probus Emesa.

Aurelian Any interesting features? Or just another stinking pisspot Arab hole?

Probus There is a temple to the sun-god. Popular in these parts.

Aurelian (*looking at the sky*) Not long till dawn. When the sun's rays strike the temple, we'll begin. I get a tingle in my balls, two hours before a battle. Very nice. How about you?

Probus No.

A squad of heavily armed Soldiers – **Cato, Antoninus,**

Philip *and* **Syrus** *– enter and sit, waiting uneasily for daylight. They don't see the Emperor.*

Cato Watch out for scorpions.

Antoninus Scorpions?

Cato Yeh.

Philip Fucking Arab secret weapon.

Cato Fucking right.

Antoninus Scorpions and women. Now I've seen it all.

Philip Yeh, both got a sting in their tail.

Laughter.

Syrus *(indicating the Palmyrene lines)* Not this one. She doesn't put it about.

Cato Oh, you're full of shite, Syrus.

Syrus No, it's definite. Some of the lads caught a straggler, back at Antioch. Interrogated him. All done right professional. Said he served in Zenobia's infantry, though you'd never of guessed. Miserable-looking specimen, all bandy legs and earrings.

Philip Yeh, and his fingernails ripped off.

Laughter.

Syrus Well, what he says is – this is through a translator, like, cos he don't speak no civilized tongue – just jabbers like an ape, incofuckingherent – what he says is, this Arab, before he lost the will to live and begged to kiss the Emperor's arse, he says his Queen as he calls her is totally what's the word? – celibate. A model of chastity. Since the day she became a widow, she has never had nothing more than the saddle of a horse in between her legs, or a eunuch in her bedroom. This is a well-known fact, he says. She doesn't shag.

Antoninus What is she, frigid?

Philip Dried up and decommissioned.

Syrus No, it's energy, you see. You expend your energy, your bodily fluids, when you have it away with the opposite sex. Not her. She saves it all for fighting. Fucking coiled like a spring. Fucking killing machine. She'll cut your cock off for a trophy – hang it round her neck. Death with tits, mate, I'm telling you.

Cato You'll stand firm. But I pity the bloke who has to kill her.

Philip He's going to look a bit sick.

Antoninus Like running a spear through your mother . . .

Syrus Don't get no medals for that, eh, Cato?

They fall silent. Aurelian and Probus approach.

Aurelian Legionaries . . .

Cato (*quietly*) Officers.

The squad snap to attention.

Aurelian Did you see it?

Cato See what, sir?

Aurelian It passed among you, a moment ago.

Cato Nothing passes us without a challenge, sir.

Aurelian Are you blind? I saw it clear as day!

Antoninus The enemy, sir?

Aurelian No, not the enemy – a friend! Divine in form, and radiating fire! An image of the sun!

Cato (*puzzled*) Don't think it come this way, sir.

Aurelian I saw the god. You must have too.

Cato Yeh, well –

Probus The Emperor says you saw it.

Cato The Emp—

Syrus Hail Aurelian!

Soldiers Hail!

Aurelian A manifestation of the sun on earth. A moving spirit, a guiding light. This is a sign. Our cause is blessed.

Cato We shall not fail, then, shall we, lads?

Aurelian Not with the sun-god at our side.

Antoninus Look! (*pointing at the eastern sky*) I see something!

Cato (*uncertain*) Could be something –

Probus The Emperor says it is a god.

Antoninus The sun-god!

Aurelian Protecting us!

The Soldiers stare at the sky. Sure enough, a strange light does seem to flicker there momentarily.

Go, and spread the word. I saw the god. We cannot fail. Light in the darkness. The day is ours.

Soldiers The day is ours!

Probus Hail Aurelian!

Soldiers Hail!

Probus Move out.

The Soldiers leave at a run.

What did you see – apart from the normal corona of daybreak in the desert?

Aurelian I saw victory. And so did they. Here is the plan. When the heavy cavalry charge our centre, which they will as their opening gambit, our battalions of horses are to break and run.

Probus Run?

Aurelian Run! Retreat in disarray! And let them follow.

Probus You are ordering the imperial cavalry to break ranks?

Aurelian Yes I am, Probus, and I don't want a debate about it!

Pertinax enters.

Pertinax Emperor.

Aurelian What?

Pertinax Envoys from the Palmyrenes, sir. They make a strange request.

Aurelian Go on.

Pertinax They say the clash of arms can be avoided – that no lives need be lost. If you will –

Aurelian What, man?

Pertinax Meet Zenobia face to face. Unarmed and alone. To hear a proposition.

Aurelian When and where?

Pertinax Dawn. Out there.

*Dawn on the battlefield. Drums and trumpets sounding
as the two armies prepare. Zenobia enters with Malik,
who carries a magnificent treasure-chest, which he sets
down.*

Zenobia Will he come?

Malik I see him.

*Malik looks towards the Roman lines. Zenobia looks
away.*

Zenobia Describe him.

Malik He's the one in the purple, presumably?

Zenobia Yes!

Malik Pity. The other is tall, dark and gorgeous.

Zenobia And Aurelian?

Malik Well . . .

Zenobia He has no deformity, at least? Reassure me. It's
important.

Malik Why? You only want to kill him. He is average-
looking, of average height. A powerful step. Piercing eyes.

Zenobia That will do.

*She turns and watches as Aurelian and Probus enter
from the other side. They stop and face the Palmyrenes.*

Probus Two platoons of crossbows have you covered. I
am right behind. You have the knife beneath your cloak?

Aurelian nods.

Then give me your sword.

Aurelian hands over his sword. Zenobia gives hers to Malik.

Zenobia Withdraw.

Malik He may kill you.

Zenobia He may try.

Malik exits.

Probus She is bold, the Amazon.

Aurelian So?

Probus I don't want anything to happen to you.

Aurelian Fuck off, Probus.

Probus exits. Aurelian approaches Zenobia, who stays by her treasure-chest.

Greek?

Zenobia (*nods*) Greek. I have no Latin.

Aurelian I have little myself.

Zenobia Take a look in the chest, Emperor.

Aurelian Is it full of snakes?

Zenobia You march with impunity across my land. You lay waste my crops, butcher my herds. Your columns of crunching steel and brass turn sandy tracks to sheets of glass. You have no right to do this. Yes, perhaps it is a vipers' nest. Open it, if you're a man.

Aurelian You open it. If you're a woman.

Zenobia (*laughs*) You doubt my femininity? I have five children. How many do you have?

Aurelian None.

Zenobia I doubt your manhood, then.

Aurelian I have no wife.

Zenobia I know.

Aurelian You call it your land. It is not. It belongs to the Empire of Rome.

Zenobia Surely what belongs to the Empire is what the Empire can control?

Aurelian Which is why I am here. Your proposal?

Zenobia . . . There is no need to break up the world.

Aurelian You surrender?

Zenobia (*smiles*) No. You?

Aurelian No. I never have yet.

Zenobia These are the facts. I rule the East; you rule the West. But I hold the balance, between law and anarchy. Unless you crush me, I will drive a thunderbolt through everything you know.

Aurelian Then I must crush you.

Zenobia Open the chest. There are no snakes.

> *Aurelian kneels and opens the chest. It is jammed full of treasure, fantastic jewellery, goblets, gold. He lifts up handfuls of the stuff.*

It is for you.

Aurelian For me?

Zenobia My wedding gift.

Aurelian Love-tokens on the field of war . . . ?

Zenobia There will be no war. If we marry. If we jointly reign.

Aurelian Marry?

Zenobia Just politics. No passion.

Aurelian drops the treasure back in the box.

Aurelian This is a joke, am I right? Syrian sense of humour?

Zenobia I have no sense of humour. My son has always said. I propose a very modern marriage. No need to exchange pleasantries at breakfast; no need, Emperor, to keep your mistresses a secret, to fake love for the sake of diplomacy. We meet only for the intercourse of government.

Aurelian We run the Empire together?

Zenobia nods.

From Rome?

Zenobia Where else? And the years will pass in peace. Perhaps one day when we are old we'll find we talk as friends. Give me your hand, and it's done.

Aurelian . . . If I marry, I must consummate the act.

Zenobia Unnecessary.

Aurelian Vital. Or Rome will laugh at me. The legends of your beauty are for once not inexact. Yes . . . I could go to bed with you. My face between your legs . . . yes, I can picture it.

Zenobia That is not part of the deal.

Aurelian Oh, you will not fuck a peasant, to save the world from war? It's true what they say, then, is it?

Zenobia What?

Aurelian You have so far unsexed yourself, your snatch has turned to sand?

In a flash Zenobia pulls a knife from a hidden scabbard. But Aurelian's just as quick, and in the same instant he has his knife in his hand. They go into a clinch, each holding a blade to the other's neck. It happens very fast, there's no circling around.

Well, you'd make an obedient little wife, wouldn't you?

Zenobia You insult me. You will die. My treasure will line your burial place.

Aurelian I'll give it to the whores on the Aventine, when I have beaten you. You cannot go shopping for an Empire, cunt!

They slowly back away from each other. Probus runs on.

Probus Aurelian!

Zenobia Sound the attack!

A snap blackout, followed immediately by:

SCENE TWELVE

A huge explosion. We're in Palmyra. Smoke wafts across the stage. Porphyry staggers on. Porphyry's clothes have been partly ripped away by the blast. A breast is revealed: Porphyry is a woman. Wahballat enters, coughing.

Wahballat Porphyry? Are you safe? Are you – (*He sees her.*)

Porphyry It was the sulphur. Now I'm sure of it! Sulphur added to nitre and charcoal causes an –

Wahballat . . . You are a woman.

Porphyry (*realizing she is exposed*) Oh, no!

71

Wahballat (*angry*) Why have you deceived me?

Porphyry So that I could work.

Wahballat You are a woman. Oh, thank the sun and the moon! A woman!

He embraces her and they kiss.

Part Two

SCENE THIRTEEN

Emesa. Longinus sits on a high rock overlooking the battle which rages below. He has his pen and ink.

Longinus 'Fleet-footed Zenobia'? . . . Been done. 'Sword-swinging Zenobia'? . . . Well yes, but literal, literal. 'Death-dispensing Zenobia'? . . . Sounds like a backstreet apothecary. Oh, send me an epithet, please! (*reads back*) 'As the avenging army of Palmyrene zealots smote the Romans hip and thigh upon the gore-drenched fields of Emesa, something-something Zenobia, mighty Queen of the East, raised her standard with a something-something cry . . .' Hours! Hours on one wretched little line! They'll have changed the course of history half a dozen times before I have conquered this sentence! Composition is a curse; I should have stuck to reviewing. At least one can nod off after lunch.

Zabdas enters, dragging his bad leg up to Longinus's look-out point.

I congratulate you, Commander. The alien foe is routed. Brave-breasted Zenobia, blood-bolted from the fray, stands sovereign still on Syria's sacred soil. Ah! (*He scribbles it down.*)

Zabdas What are you talking about?

Longinus They've run away, haven't they?

Zabdas Aye, they've run away, half a day's ride they ran, and us in hot pursuit. But when our heavy cavalry, oppressed with massive armour, reined up exhausted from the chase, they turned, re-formed, and cut us down like

73

reeds. Then the Gothic legions, the killing dogs of Europe, ran screaming at our unprotected flanks. That withdrawal was a feint. Aurelian is smarter than I thought.

Longinus You wouldn't call it a victory, then?

Zabdas No, I'd call it a thrashing.

Longinus carefully crosses out all the lines he has just written.

Longinus What a waste of limpid prose. Pearls tossed at oblivion. (*He sighs and looks down.*) Those divisions down there – they *are* ours, aren't they?

Zabdas No. We've got to pull back or we're finished.

*Longinus immediately gets up and starts packing his things. Zenobia enters, with a squad of Palmyrene Soldiers protecting her. All are bloody and fatigued, some are wounded. One is a **Signaller**: his instrument a long, booming horn.*

Signaller, sound the retreat!

Zenobia (*angrily*) On whose orders?

Zabdas On my orders, Majesty. We are defeated. We must regroup in Palmyra.

Zenobia We are not defeated! Not while I can fight!

Zabdas You cannot fight their shock troops on your own.

Zenobia Zabdas, has your backbone turned to jelly? I countermand your order!

Zabdas We will be encircled in a minute! Signaller, do as I say!

Zenobia What is the matter with you? Are you defying me?

74

Zabdas (*aside*) Oh, you notice?

Zenobia We go onwards! Never back!

Zabdas We go where I say, in battle.

Zenobia Come here! – and let me smash your other leg! If you want to desert, you can crawl!

Zabdas (*aside*) I have crawled for long enough. (*to Zenobia*) Your orders are ill-judged, and I won't obey them. If we fall back to Palmyra we can sit out their siege. They will never survive in the desert.

Longinus There's a phalanx of archers, marching up my hill. They are priming their crossbows. They're Romans!

Zabdas Right, move out!

Zenobia Stand and fight!

Zabdas (*to Signaller*) Sound your horn, man!

Longinus Run!

Zenobia (*to Zabdas*) I will have you crucified for this!

As the Signaller blows his horn, and all except Zenobia begin to retreat off the hill, a hail of arrows rains down on the stage. The Signaller is killed instantly. Zenobia is hit in the upper thigh and falls.

Zabdas Guard the Queen!

The remaining Soldiers, holding up their shields, manage to pull Zenobia off. The Signaller remains where he fell.

Her precious life! Protect her!

All exit amidst a tumultuous noise of battle.

SCENE FOURTEEN

Aurelian outside Palmyra, mopping his brow in the desert heat.

Aurelian What a beauty. Look at her. Enough to make you come in your sleep! What a piece of work . . . A defensive wall that size, encircling the city? How many men? How many days? With a fortification like that, they can hold out for months. Years maybe. While we catch rats in the desert. I will bring up my mantlets and slingshots of fire; my mangonels will rain death on their children. But still they have this wall.

And the tigress, caged inside it. Who seeks to humiliate me.

There must be a way . . . When I shut my eyes the sun's still there. It's burnt a path into my brain and made my skull its orbit. Inextinguishable, yes, invincible, the sun, their god of life. I will claim it for Rome. I will be the sun unconquered.

SCENE FIFTEEN

Palmyra. Night. Zenobia lies on a couch; Zabdas kneels at her side.

Zabdas They withdrew at dusk. The wall was not breached. There are many dead and wounded. But the wall was not breached. Zenobia . . . you and I have fought skirmishes of our own, for which I find I shed unfamiliar tears. I have never meant to offend you. I love you more than the beat of my own pulse. And you proposed – aye, proposed! – to a Roman! And would have married him! I am torn down. I am rubble. Please, as a memento of my aching heart, accept this little token of my love.

He offers her the cochlis brooch. Pause. Zenobia doesn't move. Then she snores lightly. Zabdas sighs, then hides the brooch as Malik leads in Wahballat and Yedibel.

Yedibel Where are her physicians?

Malik She will have no physicians!

Zabdas (*approaching them*) She sleeps.

Yedibel Sleeps? Or is she dying?

Malik (*upset*) The wound is inflamed! It weeps! I can do nothing for her.

Zabdas Not dying, please!

Yedibel We will all be butchered!

Wahballat Porphyry could treat her.

Zabdas Yes – that boy has a gift!

Malik She won't see him, Commander! No man, she says, may touch so delicate a place.

Yedibel We could go over to the Romans – ?

Zabdas No! The Queen will live! (*to Wahballat*) Majesty, speak to your mother. (*to Malik*) Have Porphyry brought here at once.

Malik leaves at a run. Wahballat goes to Zenobia's side. Meanwhile Zabdas pins Yedibel against a wall.

And *you* – never let me hear you talk of treason! I will cut out your liver and feed it to my dogs, if you betray Palmyra!

Yedibel The Queen hates the sight of you, Zabdas.

Zabdas (*downcast*) She does, aye, she does. But you have her ear. You could bring your influence to bear – when she recovers – mention my good points, that sort of thing?

Yedibel Yes, I think I can do that, Commander, yes . . . for some small consideration . . . yes.

Zabdas gives him the cochlis brooch.

Zabdas This should be enough to remind you of my qualities.

They exit. Wahballat gently wakes Zenobia.

Wahballat Mother. It's Wahballat. How do you feel?

Zenobia (*drowsily*) Are we besieged?

Wahballat Yes. But Zabdas says they can't last out for long. They have no supply lines. They'll starve.

Zenobia If Zabdas had any guts, we'd not be captive in our own city.

Wahballat But Zabdas –

Zenobia Zabdas is a traitor! We should have fought on! (*groans*) Oh . . . it hurts, it hurts . . .

Wahballat The wound is rancid. It will kill you.

Zenobia It will not kill me, don't be absurd.

Wahballat It will kill you, mother. But there is someone with a cure. A doctor. Not a man.

Zenobia Not a man? What is it, a witch?

Wahballat Look here, I'm trying to save your life! Porphyry is coming.

Zenobia I said no men!

Wahballat Porphyry is a girl.

Zenobia A girl? . . . Why does she disguise herself?

Wahballat She's a scientist, mother, and a jolly good one, too. Women are not allowed to practise science, neither here nor in Athens. So she pretends to be a boy.

Zenobia Watch your step. Who knows what other counterfeits the imposter's capable of.

Wahballat She has a true heart.

Zenobia And a false face.

Wahballat But will you see her?

She indicates that she will.

Malik!

Malik enters.

Send in Porphyry, please.

Malik makes a sign. Porphyry enters. Malik exits.

You have your bag of medicine?

Porphyry Yes.

Wahballat Use all your skill.

They touch hands for a second, and Wahballat leaves.

Zenobia My son says you are female. Prove it.

Porphyry takes Zenobia's hand and puts it between her legs.

So you have soft, moist places too. You bleed. You can bear children.

Porphyry Yes.

Zenobia But you don't paint your cheeks, nor dab scent on your wrists.

Porphyry No.

Zenobia Examine my wound. You dissemble well. I was fooled. Your master too. And poor Wahballat brought to a crisis of sexual identity. I take a rather dim view . . . (*She indicates that Porphyry should explain.*)

Porphyry My work is important to me. Wahballat understands.

Zenobia Do you love him?

Porphyry Yes.

Zenobia Enough to give up your work?

Porphyry . . . Must it come to that?

Zenobia My son must have a wife. He must breed, or why, tell me, why have we bothered? If you adore him so terribly much, and he likewise dotes on you, well, we'd better have a wedding, hadn't we?

Porphyry Are you jealous of us?

Zenobia Jealous?

Porphyry Of two people in love.

Zenobia You think that, do you?

Porphyry The glint of cruelty in your eyes. (*examining her*) Is the arrow-head inside?

Zenobia No. I cut it out.

Porphyry I will put on this ointment. It's a by-product of the crystallization of seaweed, that I've treated with essence of sulphur. An iodide, if you want the technical term. Brace yourself. It will hurt.

Zenobia Not as much as running from the Romans.

Porphyry treats the wound.

Tell me about your master. I think he dissembles too. I would have thought the man who wrote *On the Sublime* could have come up with something rather better than the eight pages of sub-Homeric doggerel that so far constitutes the history of my life, wouldn't you?

Porphyry Keep still, please. Longinus is a good man.

Zenobia There are no good men.

Porphyry He tries hard.

Zenobia He has tricked me, hasn't he?

Porphyry is silent.

If he discovers your sex, you know, you cannot remain as his pupil.

Porphyry Please . . . Majesty . . .

Zenobia No more work. No more philosophy. Just cooking, and a brat clamped on your nipple.

Porphyry I can't give up now! I'm so close!

Zenobia Then answer my question. And I will keep silence. We can reconsider the matter when Wahballat comes of age. Did Longinus write *On the Sublime* or did he not?

Porphyry (*sighs*) No, he didn't. The manuscript turned up in a library in Athens, and I made a fair copy.

Zenobia So who's the true author?

Porphyry Nobody knows. It's over a hundred years old.

Zenobia . . . A fraud. And I took his advice!

Porphyry (*dressing the wound*) This must be dressed with a fresh poultice three times a day, and I will prepare a potion that I want you to drink. I hope it will prevent the infection from spreading.

Zenobia You mean it might on the other hand kill me?

Porphyry My art is in its infancy. But I don't think you will die, Majesty.

Zenobia I assure you I will not! (*She manages to stand.*) How long till dawn? (*Calls*) Captains! Report!

Yedibel enters with Malik and Wahballat.

Yedibel Majesty, a letter from the Emperor!

Zenobia Read it.

Yedibel 'From Aurelian, Emperor of the world, to Zenobia and her allies in war. I command you to surrender. If you do so your life, Zenobia, shall be spared, and together with your children you shall live in a place of my appointing. Your jewels, your gold, your silver, your silks, your horses and your camels shall be forfeit to the Roman treasury; otherwise our enmity shall be forgotten, and the people of Palmyra may preserve their rights as citizens of Rome.'

Wahballat What do you make of it?

Zenobia He's bluffing. His horses are dying; they won't eat camel-thorn. His men are plagued by insects, and delirious in the sun. He has no friends in the desert. Yedibel, what form of reply do you advise?

Yedibel Well, er, the prospect of not actually dying at the point of a Roman sword is, well, tempting, Majesty, but –

Zenobia But you will not die if he goes away. Not immediately, that is.

Yedibel Quite so, Majesty, and my advice to you is that the imperialist aggressor must be resisted; the small nation's voice must be heard.

Zenobia Oh, my voice will he heard. It will ring in his ears for the rest of his days.

Wahballat . . . I see we're feeling better. Thank you, Porphyry.

Zenobia This youth is not like other men. His touch is free of indelicacy. His company pleases me. (*to Porphyry*) I appoint you Royal Physician. I want to see you every day. (*She dismisses Porphyry with a wave of her hand.*)

Porphyry (*bowing*) Majesty. (*She exits.*)

Zenobia Yedibel – our allies stand firm?

Yedibel The Armenians lost an entire squadron in this morning's raid, but yes, yes, otherwise they are solid.

Zenobia Ensure they're well supplied. We can't afford to lose our friends. Will the Persians support us?

Yedibel They cannot decide. They have no love for the tribe of Odainat.

Zenobia Send another runner. With coffers full of gold. Now leave me. I have a letter to write.

Wahballat Shall I call Longinus?

Zenobia No. I will do it.

   Wahballat and Yedibel exit. Malik brings a pen and parchment to Zenobia's couch.

. . . What shall I say to him, Malik?

Malik Well, I think you can skip enquiring after the health of his relatives and so on and so forth –

Zenobia Malik.

Malik I myself would first decide the colour of the ink. If you want to infuriate the silly old tart, I'd suggest a regal purple. If you want to vent your anger, a vile, splenetic red. Blue will look cool and commanding, unmoved by his arrogant tone. Black for death, as in his. Green to deceive him, and imply you've lost your wits. Everything rests on your appraisal of the man's personality.

Zenobia I rather liked him, as a matter of fact.

SCENE SIXTEEN

Night. Aurelian enters his tent.

Aurelian Bring my breastplate! Hone my sword! With one stroke I'll finish it, and we can all go home! I will shaft her, good and hard, right up to the hilt.

Probus, Pertinax and the Prefect enter. Probus has Zenobia's letter.

Probus No, I don't think so.

Aurelian But she requests it! Single combat! She's begging to be slain!

Probus She knows it is not politically possible for you to accept.

Aurelian I don't give a toss about politically possible – I want to win! Victory is victory, isn't it? Come *on*, Probus!

Pertinax You might lose.

Aurelian Bollocks!

Probus I have seen her with a knife-blade at your throat.

Pertinax She is strong, and quick.

Probus And devious.

Aurelian And I am old and knackered, my sword-arm limp and flaccid, drooping like a geriatric's prick, this is what you're telling me? You're telling me I can't win a fight with a slag in a sandpit? What's she going to do,

84

scratch my fucking eyes out? Fuck it, you lot are losing your edge. Are we soldiers, or poofs in fucking armour?

Probus Nobody is questioning your martial expertise. Your skills put our finest gladiators in the shade. But I hardly think, Emperor, that butchering this upstart will bring us the accolades we long for. I hardly think that winning a war this way will speed the course of your inevitable deification.

Aurelian It is not just a war. It is the reunification of the world. I can live with a little shame.

Prefect If you kill a woman, Emperor, the victory is tainted. We will march home with our tails between our legs. Our wives will turn to icebergs in our beds, and watch us with misgiving in their eyes. And if you – say you stub your toe against a stone – the sun blinds you for a second – she gets in a lucky blow – where are we then? No, this action must be decided by military might, not a degrading tussle between the Emperor of Rome and some Syrian courtesan. We're not in ancient bloody Greece, with minotaurs and fuck knows what; this is as you say a war for the preservation of civilized society. So do it the civilized way.

Pertinax Besides, how do you know you can trust her? What if she comes with hunting dogs, tigers, birds of prey that know her call? What if she does magic?

Aurelian Magic?

Prefect Oriental witchcraft.

Aurelian Fuck, I hadn't thought of that. Strange practices they have here . . . strange fruit . . . the heat, the incense . . . invading your brain . . .

Probus Sir, this letter scripted in ridiculous gold leaf is designed precisely for the effect it has achieved. We are suddenly unsure of ourselves. She means, with this hysterical gesture, to undermine our morale. Don't give her the pleasure.

Aurelian I would give her the pleasure of a fist up her arse.

Probus We all would.

Pertinax Bit of luck we all will.

They laugh. Aurelian relaxes.

Aurelian All right. What's the alternative?

Prefect I've got a deal going with some Arabs, the Tanukh I think, not the locals, nomads. No allegiance to Palmyra. They will guard the supply routes back to Antioch. For free use of Zenobia's wells, when we liberate the city. No jewels, no gold. Just a drink for the camel. Any good?

Aurelian Well done. Give them the water, Prefect. If it means we can eat.

Pertinax I think we should fight at night.

Probus At night? No one does that.

Pertinax Exactly. Bring up the battering-rams under the stars. Disconcert the fuckers.

Aurelian I like it. And we'll play music.

Pertinax Music?

Aurelian Marching music! All night long! Be like trying to sleep on a parade ground! – Probus?

Probus The Armenians are wavering. Give them a push, and they'll turn. They owe nothing to Zenobia. If we pay more, they'll fight for us.

Aurelian Do it.

Probus What about the Senate?

Aurelian A pissing contest in a public bath. I'll deal with
the Senate, don't worry. Pay what the Armenians ask.
We're going to break this bitch. Here's something odd that
happened. I went into the temple, you know, on the
acropolis at Emesa, temple of the sun. Temple of
Heliogabalus. Beautiful fucking thing. Stained glass like a
mermaid's tears, and the last of the light coming through
. . . beautiful. I saw it again.

Probus The vision?

Aurelian Great shimmering ball of flame, streaks of pure
fire all around it. I went down on my knees. It floated.
Over my head, as I prayed. I was not harmed. I was
favoured! The sun-god fights beside us. We will worship,
every dawn.

Prefect I have seen it too. I think I've seen it. And some of
the men.

Aurelian One light, in the heavens. One force, and that is
us. When we smash this wall . . .

SCENE SEVENTEEN

*Wahballat's library. Night. He and Porphyry lie on the
floor, on a makeshift bed surrounded by books. A tray of
food nearby. The insistent sound of the battering-rams,
hammering at the walls, and Roman martial music far in
the distance.*

Wahballat Happy?

Porphyry Yes.

She kisses him.

Wahballat It's puzzling, isn't it? Outside a war is raging, men cascade in blood. Yet here I am in paradise. The happiest days of my life. No system of philosophy can explain this to me.

Porphyry When you find the one person in the world that you want to be with . . . that you can share things with . . . all the rest is vapour, swirling gas . . . The battering-rams are your pounding heart, the missiles air-borne kisses . . . Put you and me together, gently heat, and look: essence of love.

Wahballat Our love is doomed.

Porphyry Don't say that.

Wahballat How long can they (*the Romans*) keep it up?

Porphyry For ever. I don't care.

Wahballat The sky will crack open, and the wells will run dry. It's finished. Palmyra is dying.

Porphyry But we have our work! Let them make history; they are insects, scrabbling in the dung. We are close to our goal. The medicine worked on your mother; the formulae fall into place. As long as the walls keep the Romans out, we can sift through the secrets of matter. And soon we will have knowledge, of everything and nothing, and we will look down on their bickering like bored, impassive gods!

Wahballat But it's my home.

Porphyry I am your home. Come inside me and be safe.

Wahballat My love . . .

> *They kiss. A secret door in the bookcase creaks, sticks, and starts to open.*

Porphyry What's that?

Porphyry and Wahballat leap up as Timagenes enters through the secret door.

Wahballat You may not enter!

Timagenes pulls a knife. Porphyry and Wahballat back away. Timagenes sees the food, and falls on it, eating ravenously.

Timagenes Do you see where your lethargy has brought us? There is no food out there! But the dictator's son does not go hungry.

Wahballat How did you get in?

Timagenes There are passageways hidden throughout the palace. Tunnels, underground bunkers. I know them all. You must act now, before it's too late!

Porphyry What does he want you to do?

Wahballat Stage a coup against my mother.

Timagenes Take command! Negotiate a truce!

Porphyry (*to Wahballat*) No, you can't! The Romans will not let me work! I need Zenobia in power!

Timagenes Wahballat, don't listen! Call a halt to the killing!

Porphyry But I'm so nearly there! The ancient doors swing open! Oh, Wahballat, don't ruin everything we've struggled for!

Timagenes A bloodless revolution, that's all – and the westerners will leave us in peace.

Wahballat (*torn*) Give me room to think!

Timagenes There is no time! How can you sit here reading books, blind to the catastrophe of a once great city?

*Timagenes grabs Porphyry and holds the knife to her
throat, backing away towards the secret door.*

The boy comes with me, until you come to your senses!

Wahballat Let her go!

Zenobia enters, completely recovered from her wound.

Zenobia (*furiously*) Timagenes!

*Timagenes is distracted. Wahballat throws himself at
him. Porphyry gets clear as the men struggle. Wahballat,
fighting like a man possessed, gains the upper hand. He
corners Timagenes with the knife.*

Kill him.

Wahballat . . . I can't, mother.

Zenobia Weakling!

Wahballat Timagenes is not a fool. The war is going
badly.

Timagenes Children are dying of starvation! The longer
we resist, the greater the Roman's anger will become.
Eventually they'll wear us down, and then destroy us all.

Zenobia You know nothing! What do you know? We are
winning!

Timagenes My family is under the bombardment!

Zenobia Help will come soon from the Persians!

Timagenes The Persians? You are dreaming, surely! You
have been dreaming for four years! You dream you are a
strategist – you dream you have an army – you even
dream you have the blood of Cleopatra! It is all fantasy,
Zenobia, motes of dust!

Zenobia (*drawing her sword*) Step away, I will kill him.

Wahballat stands in her path.

Wahballat Go, Timagenes.

Zenobia (*to Wahballat*) What, with a knife in your hand?

Wahballat It's how we do things now, isn't it?

Timagenes makes his escape.

Zenobia I have old men and boys on the battlements. If they can pick up a spear, they can fight. Join them.

Wahballat You didn't bring me up to be a fighter.

Zenobia Things have changed. The sky is dark with their arrows. Their battering rams are rattling my teeth! I need help!

Porphyry We are scientists. We have no interest in the art of war.

Wahballat Leave us.

Zenobia (*in a fury*) Yedibel!

Zenobia exits. Porphyry is already back at work.

Wahballat Gosh, I didn't know I could do that.

Porphyry Our time is short. Prepare the chemicals.

SCENE EIGHTEEN

Aurelian, Probus and the Prefect stand looking up at the wall. The battering-rams and martial music continue in the background.

Prefect Why do these bastards always resist? Why don't they accept the inevitable?

Aurelian Perhaps they've forgotten we're here.

Probus . . . We need new weapons.

Prefect Nothing wrong with our weapons.

Probus They're predictable. What we do is always predictable. Here's our attack, here's their defence. We've done it for hundreds of years! They resist because they know how to resist. We need something against which resistance is simply unimaginable.

Aurelian What's on your mind, Probus?

Probus I'm not sure, sir. A weapon of destruction. There is so much destruction in nature. The power of the lightning bolt, the blast of the volcano . . . ! If we could harness that, we'd soon demolish their brickwork.

Aurelian I like it when young men dream.

Probus (*pointing*) An explosion, there, at our command! Pow!

Aurelian It's never going to happen.

Prefect I've been using battering-rams for my entire career and they haven't let me down yet.

Probus But one day, we will be beaten.

Aurelian frowns thoughtfully at Probus.

SCENE NINETEEN

On the walls of Palmyra. Yedibel looks down. Longinus joins him.

Longinus She wishes to see me?

Yedibel Those soldiers below.

Longinus The ones marching out of the gates?

Yedibel Know who they are?

Longinus Not definitively.

Yedibel They are Armenians. Our chief allies. They are changing sides.

Longinus Ah.

Yedibel You spoke for war, Longinus. Your current position is unenviable. For a small remuneration, I will try to save your life.

Longinus What do you want, Yedibel?

Yedibel Zabdas, for example, gave me this.

He shows the cochlis brooch.

Longinus That's mine!

Longinus makes a desperate grab for it and they struggle. Meanwhile Zenobia, Zabdas and Malik appear further along the battlements.

It's mine! It's my insurance!

Longinus succeeds in getting hold of the brooch. He breathlessly approaches Zenobia, concealing the brooch as he goes. Yedibel follows him.

Zabdas Is it true? The Armenians have quit us?

Malik Yes! Look!

Zabdas Mercenaries! Daft to use them!

Yedibel Now we're weak on the eastern ramparts!

Malik Commander, you must redeploy!

Zabdas Now I get tips from a eunuch. This place is a madhouse!

Zenobia Longinus, you have betrayed me.

Longinus August Queen, I do not, with respect, recall being consulted about Armenians – had I been I should have informed you that they are an unreliable, self-serving race, well-known in international circles for their vacillation and –

Zenobia Not the Armenians! I mean this! (*She flourishes her copy of* On the Sublime.)

Yedibel Majesty, we must talk tactics –

Zenobia (*ignoring him; to Longinus*) You presented yourself as a philosopher of genius. But now I know you are a fraud. You plagiarized an ancient text, and claimed it as your own!

Zabdas We can fortify the palace, and hold out there –

Zenobia (*ignoring him*) I thought you were an intellectual!

Yedibel The bunkers are provisioned –

Zabdas But will we get help?

Longinus I rescued a neglected work, found gathering dust in a cellar.

Zenobia You stole it! And I look a fool!

Malik Majesty, nobody cares about the Sublime! We are all on the verge of extinction!

Zabdas I say abandon the wall!

Zenobia Never! The wall is our bedrock!

Longinus What if, a thousand years from now, I come to Palmyra, and take away the marble frieze that crowns that portico? And I set it up in a distant land, seat of some unlikely empire, and put my name on it? Who's to say who owns it?

Zenobia grabs Longinus and pushes him half over the parapet. She dangles him there.

Zenobia You counselled badly! Now I understand why!

Malik Majesty –

Longinus manages to hold up the cochlis brooch.

Longinus I know you killed your husband!

Zenobia That's my brooch!

Longinus Yes, she killed him, I was by his side when he perished!

Yedibel You killed King Odainat?

Zenobia No!

Longinus struggles to safety. Zenobia backs away from the men. Malik goes with her.

Longinus She poisoned his wine!

Zabdas This is unbearable!

Zenobia (*putting her hand to the hilt of her sword*) Well, a woman who murders her husband is a woman for men to be scared of, I would think.

Yedibel You killed him, and led us into this?

Longinus I was there! This jewel proves it!

Zenobia (*aside to Malik*) Malik – a camel – we'll go to the Persians.

Malik exits at a run.

Yedibel I am handing her over.

Zenobia Zabdas?

Zabdas I can't help you now.

Longinus We must save ourselves. Abjure her.

Yedibel She has failed her country.

Zenobia draws her sword.

Zenobia I? I have failed? I have shed my blood, I have watched my blood drain down in the soil of my native land! And you dispute my patriotic fervour? Do you not think I dream the people's dreams? Do you not know in what place you live? We had poetry before the Greeks! Architecture before the Romans! We built the first cities! Invented the alphabet! We awoke at the dawn of civilization, and you would have us lost in the sleep of history? If the name of Palmyra is forgotten, we have all failed in our duty!

Malik re-enters below.

Malik Majesty! Come!

Yedibel Take her!

Zabdas draws his sword and advances on Zenobia without much enthusiasm.

Zabdas Zenobia, please –

Zenobia swings and cuts into Zabdas's one good leg. He drops. Zenobia runs for it.

Yedibel Guards! Arrest her!

Zenobia exits with Yedibel following.

Longinus What can I do?

Zabdas (*screaming in agony*) Throw me from the battlements! Skewer me on their spears! That would fix it! This rat that gnaws at my heart. Oh, the vermin of emotion!

Aurelian's tent. He and the Prefect examine a map. An icon of the sun-god is prominently displayed. Pertinax and a Centurion bring in Timagenes, his hands bound.

Pertinax Came over to our lines. Claims he knows how to breach the wall.

Aurelian Does he, indeed? (*to Timagenes*) Who are you?

Timagenes I was First Minister in the government of Palmyra – until I fell from grace.

Aurelian And now you would have your revenge . . . ?

Timagenes I would see the war ended. My people are dying.

Aurelian Mine are dying too. So fucking what?

Timagenes I can find the secret conduits, that perforate the wall. I can show you how to take the city. It gives me no joy to do so, Emperor. Just end it, swiftly. And be merciful.

Aurelian Oh, I am merciful, my friend, I am as welcome as rain in August, to a parched and bitter land. You will lead us to Zenobia?

Timagenes Zenobia has fled, last night, upon her swiftest camel.

Aurelian To?

Timagenes To cross the Euphrates, and recruit fresh forces.

Aurelian Pertinax, take a platoon of horse, and try and head her off.

Pertinax leaves at a run.

Wahballat's library. Night. He is sleeping on the makeshift bed. Porphyry enters in great excitement, carrying a flask of bubbling liquid of the deepest red.

Porphyry (*gently*) Wahballat – wake up! Wake up, my darling . . .

Wahballat I'm so tired . . .

Porphyry You will never be tired again. Or frail, or sick. I think I've done it!

Wahballat You've done it?

Porphyry If my calculations are correct – this is the elixir!

Wahballat Are you saying . . . we can outlive the war . . . outlive the Romans? We can be together for all time?

Porphyry Try it!

Wahballat Kiss me first.

They kiss.

Would I still love you if you weren't clever?

Porphyry (*laughs*) Would you still love me if I wasn't a boy? Drink.

Wahballat (*looking at the potion*) I trust you.

Porphyry I love you. I will never hurt you. Drink.

Wahballat drinks a long draft of the elixir.

Wahballat How do we know if it works?

Porphyry Ask me again in a hundred years.

Wahballat Now you.

98

Porphyry takes the flask. But before she can drink, a squad of Roman Soldiers bursts into the library. They rush at Porphyry and grab her. She struggles. The flask is dropped to the floor and smashes.

Cato Got one!

Antoninus Get the other!

Porphyry Run!

Wahballat dodges the Soldiers and gets the secret door in the bookcase open. He looks back –

Run! Run!

Antoninus After him!

Wahballat exits. The Soldiers halt at the secret entrance.

Philip It's pitch black, Cato.

Syrus Could be booby-trapped .

Cato Fuck it, leave him. Now, what have we here?

Philip Books. Lot of books.

Cato Books?

Syrus (*looking at one*) Arab writing. All squiggles.

Antoninus Any pictures?

Syrus Nah.

Cato Burn them.

Porphyry No!

A Soldier hits Porphyry. Another starts to tear up a scroll.

Please! The wisdom of centuries!

Cato Put him with the others. Await orders.

Porphyry is dragged out. Syrus tries to light a tinderbox.

Get a move on, Syrus. I want to see a fucking conflagration on the count of three. One – two –

SCENE TWENTY-TWO

Zenobia and Malik on the banks of the Euphrates.

Zenobia There must be a boat!

Malik There isn't.

Zenobia Not a raft? Not a hollowed-out tree?

Malik The river's as broad as an old whore's bum. We need a ferryman.

Zenobia Am I beaten by a stretch of yellow water? (*She sits disconsolately.*) Look at it. I hate it. And over there is Persia.

Malik A boat will arrive.

Zenobia Is this how it ends, Malik? All dreams, all ambitions, all desires – just washed away? Your whole life turned to mud? I had hoped to walk through Rome in triumph. Now I sit by a river in disgrace.

Malik There is no disgrace for you, Majesty. I have served you since the day you married. I knew you by your Aramaic name, when you were nothing, just a girl from the hills. Now the whole world knows Zenobia, Queen of the East. Even in defeat, she will be remembered.

Zenobia I am not defeated yet, believe me!

Malik They have all abandoned you. But you must survive. You have so much to offer. Your beauty, and your will. A beacon for all women, for all time. You must survive.

Zenobia How can I reward you, Malik?

Malik I just want to see you happy . . . Look! A boat! (*waves*) Over here!

Zenobia When I've crossed the Euphrates, I'll be happy.

Offstage, Pertinax and a squad of Roman Soldiers arrive.

First Soldier (*off*) There!

Second Soldier (*off*) By the river!

Pertinax (*off*) Take her alive.

Malik (*to the ferryman*) Hurry!

Pertinax and the Soldiers run on and surround the Palmyrenes.

Zenobia I've always hated rivers.

Pertinax I arrest you in the name of Imperial Rome!

Zenobia I hate the sea too.

Malik Here they come, the tourists, looking for their souvenirs.

Pertinax Kill him.

Malik Oh, kill me in a moment. First I must dance for my Queen.

Malik dances and sings, a reprise of his earlier number. Zenobia watches with tears in her eyes. Malik dances flirtatiously in front of the Soldiers, who start to laugh.

First Soldier Fucking fairy.

The Soldiers move in on Malik from all sides, their shields held before them. At the last moment, with the Soldiers distracted, he calls out to Zenobia:

Malik Now!

Zenobia Malik!

Malik Go!

The Soldiers stab Malik, who dies. Zenobia makes a run for it, drawing her short sword. The Soldiers pursue her: two of them have spears, one has a net. She is cornered. She fights wildly, wounding one of the Soldiers, but then they pincer her with the long spears and finally throw the net over her. She screams in defiance as she is picked up and carried off.

SCENE TWENTY-THREE

Aurelian in Zenobia's palace, looking out at the city. Probus and Timagenes nearby.

Aurelian Most extraordinary town I've ever laid eyes on . . . Look at those towers! What are they?

Timagenes Burial places, Emperor.

Aurelian Bodies in the sky? Why?

Timagenes I could not say. Tradition.

Aurelian Good for you. Traditions are important. And these marvellous temples – how many gods do you worship?

Timagenes All the gods, Emperor.

Aurelian No special one?

Timagenes No.

Aurelian How curious. But I must admit I'm staggered by your buildings. And this is a royal palace, all right. Look at the ceilings! The mosaics! Fancy living here, Probus? Nothing like it in Europe!

Probus No thank you, Emperor.

Aurelian Now traditionally at this point I embark on the customary orgy of destruction and smash this place to pieces, but I can't destroy such colonnades as those, can I? Act of vandalism. I don't want to go in the books as the lunatic with the sledgehammer. So I am prepared to break with convention, and let them stand.

> *Pertinax enters with the Prefect and Soldiers carrying Zenobia in the net. They tip her out at Aurelian's feet. Her hands are bound.*

Pertinax The Queen of Palmyra is your prisoner. We got her at the river.

Aurelian What was she doing – having a paddle?

> *The Romans laugh.*

Timagenes (*to Zenobia*) Forgive me, Majesty. I did it to save lives.

> *Zenobia spits at Timagenes.*

Aurelian Now, now – no need for that. Timagenes, you have done us a service. Without you we'd be squatting in the sand from now till Saturnalia. For that fucking wall is impregnable. You have my personal thanks. However . . . I cannot love a traitor. I cannot reward a traitor. For a traitor once may be a traitor again. It's a sickness. And there's only one cure.

> *Quickly, Aurelian draws his dagger and stabs Timagenes, who dies.*

Remove him. Probus, throw your cloak over that (*Zenobia*). I don't like looking at naked women. Unless I've got my balls between their legs.

> *The Soldiers drag out Timagenes's body and Probus covers Zenobia with his cloak.*

Now leave us alone.

Prefect Not a good idea, Emperor.

Aurelian Perhaps not, Prefect, but it is a bloody order.

Probus She has the eyes of a viper.

Aurelian Out.

Probus, Pertinax and the Prefect leave. Aurelian is alone with Zenobia.

. . . Latin? I have no Greek.

She turns away from him. He smiles.

What's it going to be, then? Little torture? Little rape? Where shall we begin? (*Pause.*) Lovely place you've got. Pity I must knock if down.

Her eyes flash.

So there is blood, hot blood, behind the mask. There is a human being in there somewhere.

Zenobia drops her cloak to the floor.

Put your tits away. I'm too old for all that.

Aurelian picks up the cloak and hands it to her.

Zenobia When are you going to kill me? Don't drag it out. I hate waiting.

Aurelian Not expedient, they say. My advisors. Do you have advisors? Such a pain in the arse. But I have to leave a caution. Some trace of my displeasure. Some guarantee of order in the world.

Zenobia We could have ruled the Empire together.

Aurelian That's true. But now I have it to myself.

Zenobia And you wish to humiliate me.

Aurelian Too fucking right I do. (*thoughtfully*) Outside Antioch – saw a bloke up a pole. Some kind of mystic. Sits in a barrel at the top. They send up bread and water on a string.

Zenobia I would throw myself off!

Aurelian You would be chained. You'd dangle.

Zenobia Then all the East would rise in my revenge! The tribes would be united in their anger!

Aurelian Then I keep you in darkness. I hide you away.

Zenobia And you will dream of me. The beauty in a dungeon. My face will sour your sleep.

Aurelian Your face I will disfigure!

Zenobia No!

Aurelian Look, I have to satisfy the appetite of Rome!

Zenobia And what do they crave? A little woman in the kitchen, with a spoon in place of a sword, crushing garlic instead of mens' heads?

Aurelian Well, it might be a start!

Zenobia Just play by the rules? (*She falls to her knees.*) Please, valiant Emperor, take pity on me! I was misled, I was seduced by possibility – I was too weak to stand up to my subjects! A woman should not fight.

Aurelian Probus!

Probus enters immediately.

Have a listen to this.

Zenobia I wear my armour with shame, for I know it demeans my sex. You have vanquished me in combat, which is just, and now I ask you, if you can, to let me live in peace.

Probus Well, well, well.

Zenobia Let me cease to be a man. Give me skirts to wear! Let me do embroidery, gardening, *anything* – but please, let me survive!

Aurelian (*in a sudden fury*) Have you the slightest notion how much trouble you have caused? Halfway round the fucking world, I came to muzzle you! And now you want to potter in your garden? I ought to cut your throat!

Zenobia I was given bad advice!

Aurelian I'll say you were given bad advice, anybody who gives that kind of advice deserves to meet a most unpleasant end!

Zenobia So, we agree.

Aurelian What the fuck do we agree on?

Zenobia They should be punished.

Aurelian Who should?

Zenobia My counsellors. My generals. Those who deluded me.

Aurelian You sacrifice your own best men –

Zenobia They caused chaos!

Aurelian – to save your worthless life?

Zenobia You must leave a caution. Rome's laws have been flouted. We had no king, no manly authority – but now you have come to discipline the wayward. You bring calm to a frenzied land. I welcome you.

Probus (*aside to Aurelian*) Cock, certainly, Emperor, but highly expedient cock. We need bodies to be picked at by the crows. And our troops can be men again, husbands again, keepers of women.

Pause.

Aurelian . . . What are their names?

Zenobia Yedibel, head of the government. Zabdas, commander-in-chief. And Longinus, a Greek, whose lust for war began the whole adventure.

Aurelian (*to Probus*) Wheel them in.

Probus exits.

Aurelian When I was a boy I used to lie in the woods all summer. Not a summer like you have, not an inferno of wind and dust, but green, pleasant. I'd watch the insects buzzing round my head. Spent a long time watching wasps. We had a lot of wasps. Now the female wasp is a terrifying beast. Know what she has to do when she gets pregnant? She has to find a nice succulent spider to paralyse with her sting, so she can lay her eggs within it. But some summers, spiders are scarce. And if she can't find one, her eggs hatch inside her, and these hungry little grubs can't tell the difference between a fat juicy spider and mummy wasp's womb, can they, so they just start chewing, eating her up, sucking at her organs till she drops dead on the ground.

Zenobia So . . . What will you do with me?

Probus, Pertinax, the Prefect and Soldiers enter, leading Longinus, Zabdas and Yedibel, who are roped together at the neck. Zabdas has to be supported.

Aurelian Take you to Rome. These are the men?

Zenobia Yes.

Aurelian Zenobia says you advised her. Is this so?

Longinus Emperor, I am a scholar by trade, and not given to meddling in matters of state. Whatever advice I may have offered to that lady was of a purely philosophical nature.

Aurelian Which one is he?

Zenobia Longinus.

Aurelian Longinus, what gods do you believe in?

Longinus It is all one and the same, Emperor, all the generation of some vital cosmic force, and I'd be more than happy to go into details with you one afternoon, if your curiosity is aroused.

Aurelian The sun-god is the only deity. Heliogabalus. Who won this war for us.

Longinus Yes, that's a perfectly valid point of view, and –

Aurelian I sentence you to death.

Longinus I have to tell you she murdered her husband. King Odainat!

Yebidel It's true.

Aurelian No. We did that. Got a bit too uppity. Neutralized him.

Zabdas *You* did it?

Aurelian My predecessor. Your defence is concluded?

Longinus I have never profaned Rome!

> *Probus hands Aurelian a thin manuscript. He reads the title page.*

Aurelian 'The Chronicle of Zenobia, Queen of the East, together with an account of her glorious stand against an evil Empire. By Cassius Longinus, scholar, of Athens, latterly resident in the maternal bosom of fair Palmyra.' (*to Probus*) Execute them on the palace steps. And get a decent crowd.

Probus Prefect.

As the Prefect starts to march the Prisoners out, two Soldiers enter with Porphyry captive.

Prefect Eagle-bearers of the Third Legion, report!

Soldier It's a girl, sir. Cut its hair off. Says it's the servant of the Queen, and demands to be brought here.

Aurelian A girl?

Porphyry Yes.

Longinus You're a girl?

Porphyry As you can see.

Longinus Well, that explains your lack of concentration!

Aurelian Speak.

Porphyry I am the Queen's handmaiden. I have served her all my life. I bathe her feet in goats' milk; I beautify her eyes. I tried to escape dressed as a boy; but now I am caught, I must serve my mistress. She needs me. Let me go with her, to the very end.

Aurelian This is your maid?

Zenobia She is devoted to me. I must have her. Bring her with me to Rome.

Aurelian You can't have a bath on your own?

Zenobia No.

Aurelian Fuck it, Probus, this is turning into a charade. They'll be packing their underthings next. (*to Zenobia*) All right. (*to Probus*) Let's do our work.

All exit except Porphyry and Zenobia. Zabdas reaches out to touch her but is pulled roughly away.

Porphyry Thank you.

Zenobia You saved my life. I save yours.

Porphyry You could not save Zabdas?

Zenobia Why should I?

Porphyry He's been in love with you for twenty years.

Zenobia In love with me?

Porphyry I think I gave him some bad advice.

Zenobia Zabdas . . . ? No, not Zabdas . . .

Zenobia weeps. Porphyry comforts her.

SCENE TWENTY-FOUR

Palmyra. Wahballat moves furtively through the city.

Wahballat I've got to find her. Perhaps she escaped! How can I live without her?

A squad of Roman Soldiers marches through. Wahballat hides until they are gone.

They burnt the library! Smashed the apparatus! All our discoveries, lost! But all the palaces still standing. They shit on learning, but have respect for wealth. This is the grandeur of Rome.

He comes upon Longinus, Yedibel and Zabdas. They have been crucified (not with nails, with ropes). Longinus has been hung upside down. All three appear dead.

. . . My tutor. Poor, equivocating Longinus. Could all your philosophy not save you? And Yedibel, the man who said 'yes'. And Zabdas? Why did we let the winds of war gather such insane velocity? A curse on my maniac mother, who brought down this blood-storm in the desert!

As he speaks, Wahballat sees that dangling on a cord from Longinus's neck is the cochlis brooch. He takes the cord from around his head and stares at the brooch, seeming to recognize it. Zabdas is still alive.

Zabdas Say nothing against her.

Wahballat Zabdas!

Zabdas The greatest Queen our land has ever seen. I loved her, Wahballat.

Wahballat I love Porphyry – who's not a chap, you know.

Zabdas She is taken to Rome with your mother.

Wahballat Rome!

Zabdas They have gone. They left a garrison.

Wahballat But why did they take Porphyry?

Zabdas Your mother asked for her. Wahballat – I am dying. I must confess to you.

Wahballat Confess what? That you loved my mother?

Zabdas No. That I killed your father. I poisoned Odainat.

Wahballat But – you were his friend!

Zabdas I coveted his wife. I thought she would be mine. But I lacked . . . something. What did I lack?

Zabdas dies. Wahballat looks at the brooch.

Wahballat This was my father's. My mother gave it him. She is to blame for everything! I should open my veins and let her sap run out! She has stolen my love from me! And somehow, some day, I will have revenge.

Wahballat exits, with the brooch.

Rome. Gratus and Quintinius, holding garlands of flowers.

Quintinius Why has the Pannonian goblin summoned us?

Gratus No idea.

Quintinius I'm a busy man. I should not be at every bastard's beck and call. Just because he won a few battles. We in Rome have had our share of grief – do you see the price of pipework has gone up? And here's me trying to install thirty heating systems before winter sets in!

Aurelian and Probus enter, still in their military uniforms. The Senators bow.

Aurelian Senators.

Gratus We greet you with garlands, Aurelian, Conserver of the World! The Empire is secure from East to West. You have worked wonders in a few short years.

The Soldiers accept the garlands.

Aurelian I asked you here because I need your assistance.

Quintinius Delighted to be of service, Emperor.

Aurelian Quintinius you're a builder, right?

Quintinius Well no, not personally – I mean I don't get muck on my hands – but I have a little outfit, yes –

Probus – refitting half of Rome.

Aurelian I have an Imperial Commission for you.

Quintinius (*thrilled*) Emperor!

Aurelian I want to build a wall.

Quintinius Garden wall? Wall to hang pictures?

Aurelian A wall around the city. A fortification.

Quintinius Phew! Take a few days to do an estimate.

Aurelian No need for an estimate.

Quintinius Always have an estimate. So the customer knows where he stands.

Probus In this case, there is no need.

Quintinius Why not?

Aurelian You're paying for it.

Quintinius I'm what?

Aurelian As a gesture of revitalized civic responsibility, you are offering your services to the public good. We need a wall. The Juthungi and Allemani are beaten, for now; but they may come out of their forests again.

Probus And who knows where the next threat will arise?

Aurelian We must be prepared.

Quintinius Er, I might have to refuse this contract, Emperor, as we have a heavy run of orders just at present.

Aurelian Then I will put you on trial for embezzlement. I can prove your involvement in the scandal at the Mint.

Probus Documents with your signature. Testimony of the staff.

Aurelian My people have been working, whilst we have been away. Now, a team of surveyors is waiting outside. They will give you the specifications. Thank you for your generous co-operation. Oh, and Senator – do a lovely job.

Quintinius leaves, downcast.

You're very quiet, Gratus.

Gratus I'm not a businessman at all. I just give parties, really.

Aurelian (*smiles*) From you all I need is advice.

Gratus Oh – excellent.

Aurelian I have brought back Zenobia, Queen of Palmyra. I have her in a dungeon on the hill. Thought you might like a peep in through the bars.

Gratus That would be a very considerable fillip, Emperor, thank you.

Aurelian Thing is, I have to work out what to do with her. I can't kill her, obviously.

Gratus No, no.

Aurelian And yet, I have to demonstrate that I will not have people snap at my bollocks with impunity. An example must be made.

Gratus Quite so.

Aurelian Well, you have experience of these affairs. You dreamt up revels for Gallienus. Very artistic, so I hear. Me, I'm just a soldier. I wouldn't know a wild bacchanalian jamboree from a kiddies' harvest festival. I like to stay at home.

Gratus I think you're thinking of a Triumph.

Aurelian Am I? Yes, I think I am.

Gratus An exquisite parade of the conquered and their rare, exotic treasures, through all the major thoroughfares of Rome. A monumental statement of our health and wealth and power.

Aurelian Sounds fucking marvellous.

Probus Organize it.

Aurelian and Probus exit quickly.

Gratus (*sighs*) I don't think I heard the magic words 'Reimbursement for your trouble'. I don't think a budget was discussed. Oh, why is there a shortage of good assassins whenever you really need one?

SCENE TWENTY-SIX

Zenobia's house of imprisonment. She enters wearing her armour, and bedecked from top to bottom in the most magnificent jewellery, very like that which she offered to Aurelian. But she is also shackled hand and foot with enormous golden chains, too heavy for her to lift on her own. Porphyry, now dressed as a girl, follows behind to help carry the chains. The sound of a restless crowd outside. Gratus enters, fussing like a couturier.

Gratus Divine, utterly divine. Never seen anything like it! Cost me an absolute packet, but who could place value on a spectacle like this? Your beauty alone is worth the outlay.

Porphyry How long will it take?

Gratus Nine hours. First come twenty elephants, and two hundred more ferocious beasts, including four tigers, and, I believe, a giraffe. Eight hundred pairs of gladiators, for the Colosseum tomorrow. And then the prisoners, and you. Immediately behind you is the Emperor, in a chariot drawn by four stags, which once belonged to the King of the Goths. When we reach the Capitol, Aurelian will slay the stags as an offering to Jupiter. The entire army marches past and, lastly, rather as if we were prisoners too, I regret to say, the full body of the Senate. It is a triumph without parallel, and it is Aurelian's.

Porphyry Afterwards, what happens to her?

Gratus Nothing ill, I sincerely hope. This public abasement I think should be enough. We are justly famed for our parades, but also for our hospitality and, yes, gracious living.

Aurelian and Probus enter. The Emperor wears a purple tunic embroidered with palms, covered with a purple toga embroidered with stars. On his head a laurel wreath.

Aurelian Gratus, you've surpassed yourself.

Probus Let the people marvel at the enemies of Rome. Let them see what monsters we have tamed.

Gratus This lady is no monster, I am sure.

Aurelian You should have seen her on the field at Emesa. Are we ready?

Gratus One more thing.

Gratus takes a crude placard with 'Zenobia' written on it and hangs it round her neck.

Aurelian How does it feel? You content?

Zenobia I'm still here.

Aurelian Walk.

Porphyry picks up the golden chains, and she, Zenobia and Gratus exit. A roar from the crowd.

I wait for the chariot?

Probus It's outside. A slave will stand behind you, holding over your head a golden crown, and whispering constantly in your ear that all human glory is fleeting.

Aurelian Too bloody true, boy. See you tonight.

Aurelian makes to leave.

Probus Aurelian –

Probus looks around to make sure they are unobserved, then kisses Aurelian full on the lips, and holds him close.

Well done.

Aurelian smiles fondly at Probus.

Aurelian No bastard laughed at me, did they?

Aurelian exits. An even greater roar from the crowd.

SCENE TWENTY-SEVEN

The dining room of Gratus's luxurious villa in Tivoli: three couches arranged around a table inlaid with ivory. Porphyry enters, well dressed in women's clothes. She places a vase of flowers on the table. Gratus enters.

Gratus Everything set for this evening?

Porphyry It's all in hand, sir. The wild boar is on the spit; the oysters and eels are coming from the market; the wine is opened.

Gratus Do you know how to purify wine?

Porphyry No sir, I'm sorry, I don't.

Gratus Drop the yolk of a pigeon's egg into it – it draws the impurities down to the bottom of the flask.

Porphyry That's very intriguing. Why do you suppose that happens?

Gratus I haven't the faintest idea.

Porphyry (*wistfully*) Cooking holds its share of mysteries, doesn't it?

Gratus I'm not particularly interested in cooking. It's eating I'm interested in. Have you got the African snails?

Porphyry Yes.

Gratus The walnuts and figs from the cellar?

Porphyry And the dormice in honey.

Gratus Mmm. Tell cook not to season the dishes with salt; unwashed sea-urchins are better.

Porphyry And the best ones come from Cape Misenum, if I'm right?

Gratus You're learning fast, Porphyry. The serious banquet is composed mainly of soft food, the kind that will putrefy fast. Money must be spent. A lot of important people are coming.

Porphyry I do understand.

Gratus Is she dressing?

Porphyry She looks wonderful.

Gratus Oh, how right you are. She looks magnificent, every hour of the day. I am a lucky bastard, aren't I?

Porphyry Very lucky, sir.

Gratus I am going to the Baths, so I shall be relaxed at feeding time. Please inform her. Is it raining? It looks like rain.

Zenobia enters. She does indeed look magnificent, a sophisticated Roman matron, wearing the finest silks, and make-up, and a string of pearls.

My treasure . . . My little desert bloom . . .

Zenobia kisses Gratus, then shows off her clothes.

Zenobia Will I do?

Gratus Exquisite.

Zenobia The pearls are adorable. So generous of you, Septimus.

Porphyry I will just check on the pastries.

Porphyry exits.

Zenobia Did you know Cleopatra once swallowed a pearl worth ten million sesterces?

Gratus No!

Zenobia Yes! Dissolved it in vinegar. She bet her Roman lover she could prepare a feast more costly than he might ever imagine.

Gratus She was right. But please – don't eat your pearls, my darling.

Zenobia (*laughs*) I shan't. As long as you've got me something tasty.

Gratus I have for you a very special treat. A lamprey, caught before spawning – for its flesh is softer then – and served on a bed of livers, from plaice and bass and turbot.

Zenobia And to follow?

Gratus Sow's udders.

Zenobia I can hardly wait.

Gratus Nothing is too perfect for my luscious Arab queen. I was going to the Baths but . . . you in that dress, it's just . . . you make my mouth water.

Zenobia You may do what you like with me.

Gratus May I really?

Zenobia I am your wife.

Gratus I want you.

Zenobia Yes.

> *Gratus kisses her, and gropes her lewdly. She seems to quite enjoy it. She moans a little as he kisses her passionately and buries his head in her bosom.*

Now go to the Baths. Refresh yourself.

Gratus I adore you, Zenobia.

Zenobia I know.

> *She gives him a long sloppy kiss and he leaves, blowing kisses. Zenobia is rearranging her clothes as Porphyry returns, carrying sticks of lighted incense which she places around the room.*

Porphyry You seem happy.

Zenobia I am. The cream of Roman society is coming to my table. The meal will be a dream, a work of art. The talk will be of lechery, philosophy and fashion. And the wholesale price of bricks, if Quintinius is on his usual form. Of course I am happy! My husband treats me well.

Porphyry Things have turned out comfortably.

Zenobia Things have turned out better than I ever thought possible. I live in Rome! I have a villa! Why, I have a hundred pairs of shoes!

Porphyry But the price is high.

Zenobia The past is forgotten. A miasma of heat and sand. You know what they say here? 'A happy people has no history.' Live for the present, Porphyry. We're in Tivoli. Try and have fun.

Porphyry I am trying.

Zenobia Well try a little harder, dear, you're giving me a headache. That long face. Those droopy shoulders. Why are you so distracted?

Porphyry . . . I lost something.

Zenobia Well go and look for it! Heavens!

Porphyry Yes, ma'am.

Porphyry exits. Zenobia wafts around the room, humming cheerfully to herself. Aurelian enters, in civilian clothes. She doesn't see him at first. He watches her. His head and shoulders are wet with rain.

Zenobia Emperor!

Aurelian I stood in the atrium. Nobody came.

Zenobia They're all in the kitchens. Preparing a feast.

Aurelian The fat Senator loves to entertain.

Zenobia Will you stay? Be our guest of honour?

Aurelian What are you having?

Zenobia Sow's udders. And the vulva for Gratus. His favourite.

Aurelian The man eats the cunt of a pig. How can you live with him?

Zenobia Please, stay for dinner.

Aurelian I disapprove of gluttony. This advertising of wealth, socializing for prestige. And soldiers don't dine like civilians. A biscuit and water will do me.

Zenobia But you can't eat alone!

Aurelian I will not be alone. And at your groaning tables, isn't it forbidden to discuss politics or war? I don't do small-talk. Compulsory good humour is alien to me.

Zenobia It's easy once you've got the hang of it. (*A cloud passes briefly over her face*.) Your wall is going up?

Aurelian Up and up and up. There are threats from every corner.

Zenobia But you are secure?

Aurelian I am plotted against; and I plot. A matter of time till they get me.

Zenobia I have been and admired your Temple of the Sun. It is a masterpiece. So – how to put it? – sunny.

Aurelian You can't have people worshipping any bloody divinity they choose. It makes you weak. You must unite behind one god. So I have introduced the cult of Heliogabalus to Rome. It was that or Christianity, which gives me a pain in the tits. Turn the other fucking cheek and whatnot. No, we'll go with the sun. Your boy, Wahballat.

Zenobia What of him?

Aurelian He led an insurrection in Palmyra. The remnants of your army, the Bedouins and sheikhs, rose against my legions. I sent Pertinax. Today a courier informs me he has razed the city to the ground. I thought you'd want to know.

Zenobia (*shocked*) All destroyed?

Aurelian Smashed to bits. I'm sorry. I liked it.

Zenobia The whelp! He did that on purpose. You caught him, I hope?

Aurelian No.

Zenobia You should have.

Aurelian But still we have the trade routes. The caravans plod on. Gratus should be pleased. He can still buy his cinnamon, his ginger and cloves, to stuff inside some carcass.

Porphyry enters.

Zenobia (*to Porphyry*) Palmyra has been wrecked.

Aurelian I must get home. Have a good party. I hope the wine you give this husband is less potent than the wine you gave your first.

Zenobia I did not kill Odainat.

Aurelian Well neither did we. I checked the files. His classification was positive; a staunch ally of Rome.

Zenobia Then who – ?

Aurelian An enemy? A friend? Does it make a difference?

Aurelian exits. Zenobia sits with a glazed look.

Porphyry So, some distant town is rubble.

Zenobia My home . . .

Porphyry This is your home. This is where you sleep and eat. The men lie on the couches, leaning on their left elbows, eating with their right hands, talking; the women sit at the table, and smile. I eat with the slaves in the kitchen.

Zenobia It's a system. It works.

Porphyry (*suddenly angry*) But why have you chosen to accept it?

Zenobia . . . Were I a man you would not ask. It would pose no problem.

Porphyry You are such a disappointment!

Zenobia There are walls, you know, there are limits and constraints, on what is available to us!

Porphyry I tear down walls! It's what I do!

Zenobia I build them. There's our difference.

Porphyry I'm leaving you.

Zenobia (*surprised*) You can't.

Porphyry I have heard of a secret society, here in the heart of Rome – Rome, where we thought there was no science! – a group of researchers dedicated to cutting things up, and then cutting them up again, and then cutting and cutting, down to the smallest particle – and – how far can you go? At the very end, do you find the building blocks of life?

Zenobia Have you noticed it is raining? How wonderful! It rains!

Porphyry What has happened to you?

Zenobia I just learnt to live with the weather.

Porphyry That's the one thing I don't want to learn. I'm going to find Wahballat.

Zenobia What, still, you think of *him*? Oh, my dear, I'm sorry. He's dead.

Porphyry No . . . that's impossible . . .

Zenobia The Romans killed him.

Porphyry (*screams*) No!

She runs out. Zenobia sits alone, hard and distant. After a moment she gets up and begins to go around the room, plumping up the cushions on the sofas. The sound of heavy rain.

*Palmyra. Windy. Huge chunks of masonry lie on the
ground, overgrown with weeds. The sound of sheep.
Wahballat enters, dressed as a shepherd.*

Wahballat I tend my flock. We live in huts. The desert
wind torments us. Nothing left now of the great
metropolis. Just jagged columns pointing at the sky – the
drifting sands of history. Sometimes I dream of my
alchemist lover. In the past, when I was young. But I never
grew up. Never came of age. I've tried to kill myself
several times. Pointless.

> *Two Explorers enter,* **Dawkins** *and* **Wood**. *They wear
> the clothes of Englishmen of 1750. Wood has a sketch-
> pad. Wahballat hides.*

Dawkins We've found it! God bless us, we've found it!

Wood The ruins of Palmyra!

Dawkins Start drawing, Mr Wood!

Wood It exists! It truly exists!

Dawkins The city of Palmyra . . . ! The architecture of
your dreams!

Wood We shall have etchings that will be the talk of
London.

Dawkins All those miles of nothing – then suddenly, this!
The home of Zenobia, who rose against Rome in what? –
two-seventy AD? – damn near fifteen hundred years ago!

Wood And it's ours, Mr Dawkins. We're first.

Dawkins Draw! Draw everything in sight!

> *Wood begins to sketch. Wahballat moves and they see
> him.*

A shepherd.

Wood What's that he's got round his neck?

Dawkins A gem.

Wood There's treasure here?

Dawkins (*to Wahballat*) May we take a look, sirrah? At your jewel?

> *They close in on Wahballat, who panics and tries to escape. They grab him. Dawkins rips from his neck the cochlis jewel of Odainat.*

Wood Where is it? Where's the treasure?

Wahballat (*in Aramaic*) Leave me be! I am nothing! (*He runs off.*)

Dawkins Damn! That's the end of our fortune.

Wood I believe, Mr Dawkins, these ruins will make us rich.

Dawkins You're right. Draw, man! They'll build houses in this style in Piccadilly, when they've read our book!

Wood Must have been something to see.

Dawkins Must have been a miracle. (*He gazes at the jewel.*)

Wood What will you do with it?

Dawkins I think . . . I'll donate it to the British Museum.